# HAUNTED CANADA 9

## SCARY TRUE STORIES

JOEL A. SUTHERLAND

Illustrations by
Mark Savona

Scholastic Canada Ltd.
Toronto  New York  London  Auckland  Sydney
Mexico City  New Delhi  Hong Kong  Buenos Aires

Scholastic Canada Ltd.
604 King Street West, Toronto, Ontario M5V 1E1, Canada

Scholastic Inc.
557 Broadway, New York, NY 10012, USA

Scholastic Australia Pty Limited
PO Box 579, Gosford, NSW 2250, Australia

Scholastic New Zealand Limited
Private Bag 94407, Botany, Manukau 2163, New Zealand

Scholastic Children's Books
Euston House, 24 Eversholt Street, London NW1 1DB, UK

www.scholastic.ca

Library and Archives Canada Cataloguing in Publication

Sutherland, Joel A., 1980-, author
Haunted Canada 9 : scary true stories / Joel A. Sutherland ; illustrated
by Mark Savona.

Issued in print and electronic formats.
ISBN 978-1-4431-4895-5 (softcover).--ISBN 978-1-4431-5711-7 (ebook)

1. Ghosts--Canada--Juvenile literature.  2. Haunted places--Canada--
Juvenile literature.  I. Savona, Mark, illustrator  II. Title.  III. Title: Haunted
Canada nine.

BF1472.C3S986 2019          j133.10971          C2018-906331-9
                                                 C2018-906332-7

Cover photos ©: top: Floriana/Getty Images; bottom: Narit Bualuang/123RF.

6  5  4  3  2  1      Printed in Canada  139      19  20  21  22  23

*To Tamara Sztainbok, my editor and friend, who after working on eleven books with me is only now beginning to feel a little less afraid of ghosts.*

# INTRODUCTION

This book is haunted.

It's haunted by ghosts who have walked the earth for many years and those who have been among us a short time. It's haunted by ghosts from coast to coast, in small towns and large cities. It's even haunted by the ghost of a parrot — yes, you read that right.

But what makes this book so special to me is that it's haunted by ghosts that I've wanted to write about for years. Sometimes when I uncover a particularly spooky tale I start writing it immediately, and the words flow out of me like spectres from another dimension flying through a portal. Other times I hang onto the tale for a while, not quite ready to share it with the world, waiting for the right time. For many of the ghosts in *Haunted Canada 9*, that time is now.

I've wanted to write about the ghost of Tom Thomson, a famous Canadian artist who died on Canoe Lake in Algonquin Park under mysterious circumstances — some believe murderous circumstances — for years. The same goes for the haunting of Cherry Hill House in Mississauga, Ontario.

But the story I've been looking forward to writing most is "The Legend of the Ghost Pirate," the tale of Captain Kidd and the search for his buried treasure along the coast of Prince Edward Island. My love for pirates is second only to my love for ghosts, so when I finally sat down to write that chapter I was as excited as a kid who got to ride Disney World's Pirates of the Caribbean and Haunted Mansion at the same time.

Maybe you're obsessed with pirates too. Or maybe you're more into theatre or music or canoeing or cars. All of these interests and more are covered in this book. But a word to the wise: each chapter is as scary — if not scarier — than the last. You just might find your obsession is actually your worst nightmare.

Like I said: this book is haunted. Don't say I didn't warn you.

Frightfully yours,

# THE LEGEND OF THE GHOST PIRATE

## *Montague & Bay Fortune, Prince Edward Island*

Benton Woods, who lived near the town of Montague in the early 1700s, was walking near the Brudenell River when he came across an unusual sight. Captain Kidd, the infamous pirate, had disembarked and come ashore. With long dark hair, a thick moustache and clad in red and black clothing that swirled around him in the wind, Captain Kidd was an imposing and frightening figure. The pistols, swords and daggers strapped to his body increased the dread Benton felt. He hid behind the largest tree he could find and tried his best not to make a sound.

As Benton watched from his hiding place, Captain Kidd and twenty of his crew removed a couple of large chests from their ship and dug a deep hole on the beach at the edge of the woods. It was hard work, but the crew were strong, and soon the pit was deep enough. Kidd ordered his men to place the chests inside it, then the men quickly filled it back up with sand. Content that the job was done, Captain Kidd and his crew boarded their ship and sailed off into the night.

Benton returned to his home already plotting how to steal the treasure. The chests looked incredibly heavy, and Benton knew he wouldn't be able to drag them back to his house by himself. But he didn't want to tell anyone about the treasure; he wanted to keep every single gold coin to himself. Instead he would build a small boat, sail it to the beach where the treasure was buried, dig up the chests, and drag them to his vessel and home. He set to work nearly immediately.

Working alone and in secrecy, it was a task that took Benton a considerable amount of time to complete. During that time news from England crossed the Atlantic Ocean. Captain Kidd had been captured, found guilty of one count of murder and five counts of piracy, and hanged in London on May 23, 1701.

Finally, Benton's boat was ready. He made his way back to the beach under the cover of darkness. He was careful not to be observed. Gripping his shovel, Benton leapt from his boat and strode quickly to the spot where the treasure had been buried.

But as Benton approached, he was startled and upset to find that someone else was already digging up the treasure. Benton assumed it was one of his neighbours who'd stumbled upon the secret burial location and was in the act of robbing Benton of his loot. But as he crept closer, Benton realized it wasn't one of his neighbours. Nor was it anyone living. Digging up the treasure was the ghost of Captain Kidd.

The ghost pirate spotted Benton and eyed him up and down with a look of utter contempt.

"So ye came fer me gold," Captain Kidd said. "And don't deny it, for I can see the look of disappointment in yer eyes even from where I stand. Well, yer too late, you snivelling son of a landlubber. It's gone."

Benton stood petrified, mouth wide open, silently staring at the apparition before him. The treasure was not as valuable as his life; he had already lost the one and was perilously close to losing the other.

Fortunately for Benton, Captain Kidd turned his attention back to the empty pit and quickly filled it in. Once that was done he muttered a terrible pirate oath, threw his shovel to the sand, and disappeared before Benton's eyes.

After he regained his senses, Woods walked over to Captain Kidd's shovel and picked it up. It was old and rusty. Benton turned the shovel over and discovered the Jolly Roger, the infamous skull and crossbones symbol flown by pirates before an attack, painted on the back of the blade.

What happened to the treasure — whether someone beat him and the ghost of Captain Kidd to it or Kidd himself did something to make it disappear — Benton never could say. But he didn't keep silent when it came to his encounters with the pirate. For years Benton regaled audiences, both large and small, with the tale of how he'd been confronted by the ghost of Captain Kidd. And to add an air of authority to his tale, Benton always produced the ghost pirate's shovel when he reached the climax of his story.

Thanks in part to stories like Benton Woods's, the legend of Captain Kidd's treasure being buried somewhere off the coast of Prince Edward Island has — like the pirate himself — refused to die. Every year treasure hunters journey to the island in search of gold. And many locals will admit to having dug a hole or two of their own in their youth. Few have found anything of significant value, but like Benton Woods, others have been stopped by the ghost pirate before getting very far. One of the eeriest of these accounts happened thirty kilometres northeast of Montague, in the aptly named Bay Fortune.

Around the turn of the twentieth century, Abimelech "Bim" Burke, a Bay Fortune local, met two young men who had travelled to Prince Edward Island from Boston. The men asked Bim if he knew the area well. When Bim said that he did, they revealed their plan to dig for Captain Kidd's treasure. They offered to pay Bim to serve as their guide. Bim agreed, but first he offered a piece of advice.

"It ain't no use diggin' for treasure 'ceptin at midnight," the old man said in a gravelly voice. "Anyone'll tell ya that."

The men from Boston took Bim's advice and prepared for the dig as they waited for nightfall, then made their way out shortly before midnight. They had a map of the area, tools for digging up treasure and a lantern that proved to be far more important than they could have anticipated, for that night felt darker than most. Not even a faint glimmer of moonlight managed to crack through the thick layer of clouds that blotted out the sky.

The three men tried to find the exact location of the buried treasure, but it was nearly impossible to match the map to their surroundings in the dark. But then the clouds parted and the moon lit the land in a cool blue light.

The men froze. Out on the water, now visible in the light, sailed a large pirate ship.

A small rowboat from the ship cut a path toward shore. The sulphurous smell of brimstone wafted toward land as if carried on the backs of the waves. On the rowboat were the scariest-looking men Bim had ever seen in his life. They wore handkerchiefs tied on their heads and their belts were packed with pistols and knives. Commanding the small band of pirates was Captain Kidd himself.

Without waiting for the ghost pirate and his undead crew to reach land, Bim and the other two men turned and ran back to Bim's house as fast as they could. And the two young men with dreams of striking it rich on the coast of P.E.I. headed back to Boston as soon as the sun rose the following day. They fled in such a hurry that they left behind their gear. Like many before and since, they found the risks associated with digging for Captain Kidd's treasure far too great and terrifying to be worth the potential rewards.

# THE ART OF DEATH

## *Kentville, Nova Scotia*

Walter Irving, a salesman travelling from England in the 1870s, had been told that the town of Kentville would be bustling. But he hadn't anticipated that accommodations would be so hard to come by that he'd have to sleep with the dead.

It was autumn and Walter had just travelled by train from Halifax. During the trip the conductor had informed him that a horse-racing tournament was taking place over the coming days in Kentville and that it would be difficult to find an available hotel room. As soon as Irving disembarked from the train, he saw that the streets were packed with people who had come from far and wide to attend the races. Walter had a difficult time making his way through the crowds to Wade House, the hotel he wished to stay at. His spirits fell when he entered the lobby. It was also overcrowded with people, all excitedly discussing the races they had watched that day.

Walter elbowed his way through the crowd and found the owner behind the bar. He introduced himself and asked, without very much hope, if there was a vacant room.

"I don't like to turn an Englishman away," the owner said. "And I only have one room to offer, which I would rather not put you in. However, as I said, I cannot turn an Englishman away. Have you had supper?"

Walter thought that was strange. Why should the owner hesitate to put him in a room? But he kept that question to himself and replied that he was quite hungry.

The other men in the dining room weren't interested in talking about anything but horses, so Walter ate quickly and then asked to be taken to his room. When he got there he couldn't believe his eyes. There was absolutely nothing wrong with it. In fact, it was large, beautifully furnished and had a window with a splendid view of the tree-lined street outside. Why in the world did the owner hesitate to rent it to guests?

There was a knock at the door. It was the owner, who had a request. A friend of his was visiting from Shelburne, a town on the southern coast of Nova Scotia, and he was wondering if Walter would mind sharing the room. He didn't. In fact, Irving hoped the owner's friend wouldn't be a horse race enthusiast so he'd have someone to talk with that evening. He told the owner to send the friend up when he arrived.

It was still early, so Walter went for a walk around town and enjoyed a drink or two in the hotel pub, then made his way back upstairs.

The owner's friend had already been shown into the room. Walter found the young man examining some papers when he entered, so he introduced himself and asked what his name was.

"George Cushman," the man replied. He was very thin and his face was terribly pale — so pale, in fact, that it was nearly translucent.

"Artist?" Walter asked, pointing at the drawings and sketches George was poring over.

"Only an amateur," George said with a bashful smile. "Would you like to see some of my work?"

Walter was happy for the diversion and spent the better part of an hour going through the artwork. George was really quite talented, and Walter particularly enjoyed his depictions of the Cornwallis River and the small community of Nictaux.

George told Walter to take his time if he wanted to examine them further. "Keep them all if you wish," he said, "for I'm leaving tomorrow and will probably not take them with me." He then said good night and went to bed.

Walter stayed up a little longer. He finally came to the bottom of the pile of sketches where he found one of a beautiful woman. He felt an immediate sense of déjà vu. He was fairly certain he'd seen her before but he couldn't think where. Compelled to keep the sketch of the woman, he took George up on his offer and placed the sketch in one of his cases, then returned the others to the artist's portfolio. Happy with the way the night had taken shape, he blew out the candle and went to sleep.

George disappeared sometime during the night.

When Walter awoke early the next morning and saw that the artist was gone, he began to suspect that perhaps George had robbed him. But all of his possessions were exactly where he had left them the night before, including the sketch of the beautiful woman in his case. Oddly, the door was bolted from the inside and all of the windows were locked. Walter had no idea how George had left the room.

He went downstairs for breakfast and immediately sought out the owner, telling him that his friend had departed in the middle of the night and left nothing but a single sketch as proof that he had been there at all.

The owner asked to see the sketch. They went up to the room and Walter handed it over. Upon looking at the woman, the owner fainted. Walter kneeled beside the unconscious man and splashed water on his face to revive him.

"You've been sleeping with a ghost," the owner said once he'd come to his senses. The owner's friend had not arrived as expected. George was a different soul altogether.

"George Cushman hung himself in this room," the owner said solemnly. "A young woman was the cause of it. She is now in Dartmouth, insane and in a hopeless condition."

That was it! That was where Walter knew the woman from. He had passed through Dartmouth three weeks earlier and had had some business at a mental hospital.

She had sat with her hands clasped in her lap, staring at a blank wall the entire time Walter was there. He asked an attendant about her and was told that she had been in a catatonic state since her fiancé had committed suicide.

The hotel owner filled Walter in on the rest of the sad story. George Cushman was the son of a wealthy New York businessman and had travelled north to sketch scenes of the Canadian wilderness. He settled in a room — Walter's room — in Wade House and had been especially fond of paddling a canoe out on the Cornwallis River and drawing the shoreline. But one day his canoe tipped and he swam to shore. Soaked and shivering, George was fortunate enough to be found by a fisherman named Frank Goodwin, who invited him back to his home. There George met and fell in love with Frank's sister, Alice, and the couple eventually got engaged to be married. But one night during a party, George and Alice had a terrible fight and something inside George snapped. He returned to his room alone and hanged himself that evening. The hotel owner was the unfortunate soul who had made the grim discovery the following morning.

When Alice was informed of what had happened, she screamed and ran to her room. Later, she was found sitting and staring at her wall. Hours passed, then days, then months, and she never spoke another word.

Although there was nothing to indicate that anything out of the ordinary had ever happened in the hotel room, no one ever wanted to stay there again, even those who weren't aware of what had happened there. People reported hearing strange and terrible sounds in the middle of the night: bangs and shuffling feet, moans and cries in the dark.

Not wanting to turn the Englishman away, the owner had taken a chance by placing Walter Irving there. Walter wished he hadn't. It would be a long time before he would be able to get a decent night's sleep again.

# PARLOUR PHANTOMS

## *Moose Jaw, Saskatchewan*

A young man who had been recently hired at Hopkins Dining Parlour was assigned the task of taking supplies to the basement of the building that was constructed in 1905. Although the building was old, the man had no reason to believe he had anything to fear. No one had told him the stories — not yet. Perhaps that was for the best. Then again, perhaps it was not. If he had known what was hiding in the shadows he would have been able to prepare himself.

As he was stocking the shelves with cans and jars, someone confronted him. A woman. A pale woman with no face. Terrified, the man went as white as the woman before him.

The spectre turned without a word — not surprising

since she didn't have a mouth — and floated up the stairs.

He's not the only person who has seen this ghost in the basement. Others have felt someone push them from behind on the stairs and have caught sight of the woman ducking around corners and hiding behind furniture. Some employees, like Brenda Wilson, refuse to go down to the basement unless they absolutely have to. If only the ghosts would stay down there.

Brenda is one of many people — staff and customers alike — who have had terrifying experiences in the women's bathroom on the main floor of the restaurant. One night in 1993, Brenda was alone in the bathroom washing her hands, when all of a sudden, she felt like someone was standing directly behind her. She looked up at the mirror and saw an old woman staring at her. The woman slowly faded away and Brenda ran out of the bathroom.

On another occasion, a customer was using one of the stalls when she heard the door open and the sound of footsteps entering the bathroom. As the footsteps approached her stall, the temperature dropped incredibly fast.

"It's cold in here," the woman said, but there was no response. The customer exited the stall and was shocked to find the rest of the bathroom was completely empty.

It's believed that the ghost that haunts the basement and women's bathroom of Hopkins Dining Parlour is Minnie Hopkins, wife of Edward Nicholas Hopkins. In 1882 Edward was among the first settlers who migrated west, and after travelling by train and oxen-drawn wagon, he landed in Moose Jaw and became a pillar of the community. He was elected to Parliament in 1923, oversaw the building of schools and churches, developed new trade and agricultural practices, and was responsible for creating the Moose Jaw Wild Animal Park. Edward and Minnie married in 1889 and in 1905 built the home that would one day become Hopkins Dining Parlour and a Municipal Heritage Property. They had three children, but one of them, Earle, drowned in the Moose Jaw River just two years after the family had moved into their new home. Years later, Minnie's funeral was held in what is now the restaurant's downstairs dining room — another one of her present-day haunts.

*A dining room at Hopkins Dining Parlour*

One night, after the last customer had left the restaurant, Brenda and a couple of servers completed their closing duties and turned out the lights. But the darkness was broken by a brightly burning candle, situated on a table in the middle of the dining room, that hadn't been lit a moment earlier. Before any of the staff members could ask who had lit it, all the lights turned back on by themselves, and one of the servers saw Minnie standing beside the candle. The server screamed as loud as she could and ran from the restaurant; the others followed close behind.

Another night, after the restaurant had closed, a server prepared tables for the following day, laying out cutlery, glasses and napkins on each table. She walked to the stairs but was stopped by an inexplicable sight. Much of the cutlery that she had just laid out moments before had been placed on the stairs in the shape of a cross. The next day, the server invited a friend who claimed to be a psychic to join her at work to see if she would be able to explain what had happened. They passed over the spot on the stairs where the cutlery had been laid out, and from there the friend saw the ghost of an old woman sitting alone at a table in the dining area. The ghost wore a white dress and had a long scar across her face. The friend was so upset that she couldn't remain in the restaurant a moment longer.

Many staff members have seen another spirit walk through the main floor before disappearing from sight. One night a cleaning woman was at the top of the stairs when she saw the man pass by on the main floor. Believing him to be her boss, she said, "Hi, Rick. I'm up here vacuuming." The man stopped and looked up at her, and it was at that moment that she realized he wasn't who she had thought. He was wearing old-fashioned clothing, and before he said or did anything else, he vanished.

Even children have been spooked by the restaurant's spectres. Brenda once found a two-year-old boy staring and pointing at a corner shouting, "Ghost, ghost," over and over again. When Brenda asked the boy's father what his son was talking about, the shocked father replied, "I don't know. He doesn't talk." *Ghost* was the boy's first word.

Owner Gladys Pierce's four-year-old granddaughter was seated at a table alone in the dining room one afternoon when Brenda observed that the little girl was shivering as if she was sitting in a freezer. Brenda asked what was wrong.

The girl said, "A ghost just went by."

Brenda asked, "Like Casper?"

The girl, dead serious, said, "No, a lady ghost."

You might think that, given Hopkins Dining Parlour's reputation as one of the most haunted locations in Moose Jaw, customers might opt to dine elsewhere, but not so. Not only is it a very busy restaurant, but curiosity seekers regularly visit in the hopes of encountering something unusual, something they can't explain. Some come for the history, more come for the delicious food, and others come to dine with the dead.

# ONE FINAL SONG

## *Winnipeg, Manitoba*

Jay Robbins dreamed of becoming a famous rock star. His brother, Alan, had the same aspiration and faithfully practised guitar whenever his schedule allowed. But Jay decided to try a different route to musical stardom. Shortly after he and his family moved into an old house beside St. James Anglican Church and Cemetery, Jay was overcome with the urge to learn how to play the electric organ. He purchased one with money saved from his part-time job and set it up in the basement.

The house, the family soon learned, was full of history. And some of that history lived on long after its original inhabitants had passed away. The house had been the home of one of the first Anglican priests to serve the area, possibly the Reverend William Henry Taylor. Built in 1853,

St. James is the oldest wooden church in Manitoba and is still open today.

The Robbinses appreciated that their home had played such a vital part in their community's early development, and their first days living there were happy and peaceful. That soon changed.

St. James Anglican Church and Cemetery

One evening Alan was in the second floor bedroom he and Jay shared, a pencil in hand and a blank pad of paper on the desk in front of him. Jay had gone down to the basement by himself to practise his organ and Mrs. Robbins was on the main floor in the kitchen preparing dinner. Some of Alan's new classmates had told him about something cool that he should try at home alone. They called it "automatic writing," and the process was simple enough. It involved holding a pen or pencil above a piece of paper, clearing your mind, and then waiting for a spirit to write a message with your hand. It sounded fun, exciting, maybe even a little dangerous. Alan was hopeful that he'd be able to channel a spirit and receive a message from beyond, something he could take to school the next day to show his friends.

He sat still for thirty minutes, his hand holding a freshly sharpened pencil above a notepad, willing something to happen . . . but nothing did. Not so much as a single scratch was written on the paper. Disappointed that his experiment had failed, Alan put away the paper and pencil.

But his experiment wasn't the failure he thought it had been.

All the way down in the basement, a commotion broke out. It sounded like his mother and brother were yelling at each other. Alan went down to investigate. He passed through the empty kitchen, and the sounds of the fight in the basement intensified. He also heard organ music, both beautiful and complex. It couldn't be Jay playing; he wasn't nearly skilled enough yet to be playing at such a masterful level. But if not Jay, then who?

When Alan got to the bottom of the stairs, he couldn't believe his eyes. It was Jay playing the organ, and it sounded like he'd been playing it all his life. He stared straight ahead, his eyes wide, as if his mind was elsewhere.

His back was straight and his mother was pulling on his shoulders as hard as she could. But she couldn't budge him or wake him from his musical trance.

"Stop playing!" she shouted right into his ear. "Stand up!"

Jay continued to play, neither stopping nor standing, as if he couldn't hear his mother. She and Alan were forced to stand by helplessly, too scared and concerned to be able to appreciate the beauty of the song Jay was playing.

Finally he reached the end of the song. After playing the last note, he lifted his fingers off the keys and sat as still as a statue. The glazed look in his eyes lifted and he seemed to return to his normal self. He looked at his brother and mother in confusion, and Mrs. Robbins broke the silence by telling her sons that dinner was ready.

The three of them went upstairs and ate in near silence. They hardly spoke at all through the meal, and not a word was said about what had happened in the basement.

Although he kept it to himself, Alan was certain he knew what had happened. He had summoned a spirit while trying his hand at automatic writing, although not in the way he had intended. Instead of enticing a spirit to write him a message, he'd opened a link between our world and the spirit world, allowing a ghost to possess his brother. Had it been the spirit of one of the priests who used to live in the house, perhaps the Reverend William Henry Taylor? That seemed to Alan to be the most likely explanation.

Regardless of who had slipped into his brother's body and used it to play one final song from beyond the grave,

Alan never dabbled in anything remotely paranormal again. He had learned first-hand how powerful, unpredictable and terrifying the spirit realm can be.

# PHANTOM OF THE OPERA HOUSE

## Prince Albert, Saskatchewan

Ruth Gillingham was alone in the Prince Albert Arts Centre, an old building with an imposing bell tower and a blood-red roof, as the witching hour approached. It was well past the end of her regular workday, but as the centre's program supervisor, that was occasionally part of her job. The arts centre was hosting a display of valuable gems and a staff member needed to be in the building at all hours in order to safeguard the precious stones. The doors were locked and the next staff member was due to relieve her at midnight.

*Thump, thump, thump, thump, thump.*

Someone had walked across the floor directly above Ruth's head. She was on the main floor in the office when she heard the footsteps clear as day. She guessed that a group of kids had hidden upstairs after closing time and were trying to spend the night inside, unaware that Ruth was still there.

The old wooden stairs creaked and groaned loudly as Ruth went upstairs. She searched the studio, the large space that originally served as Prince Albert's first and only opera house. All she found was some furniture and a bunch of looms covered in white sheets. No one was in the building with her. The sounds she'd heard must have been in her imagination. She went back downstairs to the office and turned her attention to her work once again.

*Thump, thump, thump, thump, thump.*

Minutes later there it was again, the unmistakable sound of footsteps from above. This time Ruth was certain her imagination wasn't to blame. Perhaps whoever was up there had hidden when they'd heard her approaching. Ruth knew she needed to brave the second floor again, but this time she wanted to make sure the intruder didn't have another opportunity to hide, so she snuck up the back staircase. She still didn't see a soul.

But what if the kids — it must be kids, Ruth continued to suspect — were hiding among the looms? It was a creepy, shiver-inducing image: children hiding under the white sheets throughout the room. Instead of checking every single loom, Ruth jangled her keys loudly and said, "Well, obviously there's no one here. Might as well lock up and go home." She then turned off the lights and went back downstairs. She sat in the darkened office facing the creaky staircase. And listened. And waited.

She didn't wait long.

*Creak, creak, creak.*

Excitement coursed through Ruth's veins. It had actually worked! Her little ruse had tricked the kids. They were coming downstairs.

*Creak, creak, creak.*

Ruth couldn't see the culprits yet but they were getting closer. Soon they'd descend far enough and she'd catch her first glimpse of them.

*Creak, creak, creak.*

The stairs continued to creak, the sound coming closer and closer to Ruth, but no one materialized. Her excitement dissolved and turned into confusion. A sinking feeling came over her.

And then — *creak, creak, creak* — the phantom footsteps reached the bottom floor. Yet there was still no one there. The sound of the footsteps could have only been created by a ghost. Ruth leapt out of her chair, grabbed her purse and keys, and fled the building. Unwilling to go back inside that night, she waited outside by the front door for the next staff member to arrive.

Another Prince Albert Arts Centre employee named John once heard the same ghostly footsteps that had terrified Ruth. It was 9:30 p.m. and he and a colleague were in a meeting room on the second floor. The building was hot and stuffy, so they'd propped open the door to keep it as cool as possible. John and his colleague heard the loud thumping sound of footsteps walking toward them, and then the open door slammed shut without warning. John and his colleague looked at each other and immediately said, "I knew that was going to happen!" They'd both had a premonition of the event a moment before it had happened.

Completed in 1893, the arts centre has been used for many purposes over the years. It originally served as Prince Albert's Town Hall and Opera House, the Prince Albert Public Library was situated upstairs for more than twenty-five years in the early 1900s, and the basement once served as a magistrates' court, complete with jail cells. It's little wonder the Prince Albert Arts Centre is known to be one of the most haunted buildings in Saskatchewan. Faces peer out through the windows when the building is empty, lights turn on and off on their own, and eerie music drifts out of the opera house when no one is inside. And Ruth has had plenty more encounters she can't explain.

*Prince Albert Arts Centre*

One night she was working late in the basement with her dog, Boots, for company. Suddenly Boots sensed that someone was in the building with them. He stood in the doorway and began barking frantically at something in the hall. Ruth tried to move past him, but the dog wouldn't be budged. She had to step over Boots to leave the room. The hallway was unnaturally cold, but Ruth had no idea what Boots saw that spooked him so much. The hall was empty.

Ruth didn't share her paranormal experiences in the building with many people. One day, when she mentioned how Boots had behaved in the basement, another staff member said it was probably the ghosts that had freaked out the dog.

"What do you mean?" Ruth asked, playing dumb.

"Oh, come now!" the woman said. "You've worked here for years. Don't tell me you don't know about the ghosts!" The woman, who had only worked in the building a short time, told Ruth that there were two lost souls trapped within it: a young woman and a middle-aged man.

Whether they're spirits who have a connection to the town hall, the opera, the jail, the library or even the arts centre is impossible to say. But however long they have been there, and whatever it is they want, the sound of their footsteps walking through an otherwise empty building is enough to scare anyone who hears them — even those with a colleague or a dog for company.

# HiSTORY COMES ALiVE

## Tofield, Alberta

It was the middle of the night and all was silent and dark. A security guard patrolled the grounds of the Ukrainian Cultural Heritage Village, a living history museum located fifty kilometres east of Edmonton. During the day, costumed interpreters portrayed the lives of pioneers in the historic buildings that had been painstakingly restored. But at night, the village more closely resembled a ghost town.

As the guard made his rounds, he heard a chilling sound coming from within the Hawreliak house — the cries of a frantic baby. Shadows moved behind the curtains of the first floor windows, but no one else was in the village. Was there a thief in the house? If someone had broken in, why had they brought a baby?

The guard had a bad feeling. Cautiously, he entered the house and stood in the front foyer for a moment to gather his courage. The baby's cries grew louder and more intense as he walked down the hall, poking his head into each room as he passed. When he peered into one of the rooms near the rear of the house, he saw a woman in old-fashioned clothing rocking an antique cradle. The guard couldn't see into the cradle, but he knew the baby's cries were coming from within it. As he approached the woman, she turned and quickly left. He followed her into the next room and immediately wished he hadn't. The woman was gone and the room she'd entered had no other exit.

The baby continued to cry. The guard returned to the adjoining room and saw that the cradle was still rocking, but now on its own. He crept toward it and stole a look inside. It was empty. He reached out a trembling hand, but before he laid a finger on it, the cradle came to a sudden stop. The unseen baby also stopped crying, as if the mother and child were afraid of the guard, unaware of how terrified he was of them.

Many people have had similar experiences in the Hawreliak house, and the most popular theory is that the ghostly mother who haunts the building is Vaselina Hawreliak. Her house was purchased and moved to the Ukrainian Cultural Heritage Village after her death in 1967. Vaselina had nine children, in whom she instilled high moral values. She was busy and hard-working, and had no patience for foul language, a fact one of the costumed interpreters of the Ukrainian Cultural Heritage Village would soon find out.

*The Hawreliak family, November 1928. In the front row, left to right, are Vaselina, Mike and Pearl. In the back row, left to right, are Ann, Kate, Nancy, Nick, Rose, Andy and Lena.*

Josh Greschner portrayed the town's British constable in the summer of 2014, and it wasn't long before he heard the ghostly rumours about the Hawreliak house. Countless employees had heard footsteps and a baby's cries, seen doors open and close on their own and chairs skitter across the floor. Some had even caught sight of the mother. Curiosity consumed Josh, so he asked a security guard, Amin, to let him explore the village after nightfall. He wanted to see if it was really as haunted as everyone said.

"It is," Amin said. "There's noises in all of the buildings. Pots and pans rattling. Footsteps."

Amin went on to share something that gave him the creeps about the Hawreliak house. "I drive past at night, doing inspections. And one time I saw lights from candles in the windows."

When Josh asked if he had gone in to check out what was happening, Amin simply answered, "I don't want to know."

Despite some reluctance, Amin eventually agreed to Josh's request to take him on an after-hours tour.

In the middle of the night, the two met up at the admin building then drove through the village. They heard the distant sound of a ringing telephone from one of the old period houses despite the fact that none of them had working phones. Amin began to have second thoughts and wanted to go back, but Josh insisted they continue. He wanted to take a quick visit to the Hawreliak house. Amin urged Josh not to go into the house, but when Josh entered anyway he followed.

Josh had been told by another employee that he should ask the "mother" for permission to enter her house. Although it had seemed like a silly notion during the day, at night it somehow made sense. He asked permission to enter and the door opened easily. The pair walked in and found the house to be empty and desolate. There was, however, a cradle in the middle of one room. Luckily, it wasn't rocking and no sound came from within.

"Finished?" Amin asked, anxious to leave.

"I need to go upstairs," Josh said. He had come this far. He had to go a little farther.

Amin refused to accompany him and waited downstairs

as Josh climbed the stairs, which creaked and groaned as he made his way up. Josh looked inside the rooms. The beds were all made and period clothing was laid out as if someone was about to rise from a deep slumber and get dressed for the day.

Amin cried out. Something on the main floor had scared him badly enough to make him curse out loud.

Suddenly, Josh heard footsteps race down the hallway and one of the bedroom doors slam shut. He tried to open it but it wouldn't budge. He'd seen enough. He and Amin got out of there. It wasn't until later that Josh was told Vaselina wouldn't tolerate cursing in her home. Although Amin didn't tell Josh what had given him such a scare, it was safe to assume that his foul language had caused Vaselina to run down the hall and slam the door, scaring them out of her house.

The Hawreliak house isn't the only building on the property that's haunted. And the mother and baby aren't the only ghosts either. Other staff members have seen salt and pepper shakers move on their own in the Pylypow house and heard ghostly tapping sounds on the windows. People have reported hearing footsteps and whispers in empty buildings, and have seen odd lights and shadows floating through the village.

Even the centre's gift shop, which isn't a historical building, is believed to be haunted. One night as a young employee was closing up, she heard the sound of heavy footsteps slowly approaching her. She looked up from her work just as a shadowy figure materialized out of thin air. It was a man in old-fashioned clothing. He silently stared at her through a glass cabinet. As fast as he'd appeared, he then disappeared. Feeling uncertain about what she'd just seen, she walked around the glass cabinet to double-check that no one was lingering in the shop. There was no one there. But then an invisible force rushed past her, spinning her around and nearly knocking her off her feet.

A few nights later she was alone once more, or so she thought. While placing glass figurines on display she heard the same heavy footsteps slowly approaching. This time they passed her. She followed the sound, and the man appeared again. After staring her down for a tense moment, he disappeared. But the woman could still hear him walk away. She followed the footsteps, turned a corner into the museum area, and caught sight of the man. He was now translucent, and he walked straight through a wall without hesitating or slowing down.

A different employee was responsible for restoring a period farmhouse. Much of her work needed to be completed after hours when the village was empty. As she swept the floor within the barn one night, she heard the sound of horse hooves on the dirt road outside. That didn't make sense. No one else was supposed to be nearby, least of all any of the historical interpreters. Confused and intrigued, she stopped sweeping and stepped outside.

She saw the same man the other employee had seen in the gift shop. He was standing in front of a wagon that was hitched to two black horses. When he spotted her, he beckoned her to get into his wagon, but he didn't utter a word. Oddly, the horses didn't make a sound either. When the man gestured for her to get into his wagon once more, the woman panicked and ran back to the farmhouse. She grabbed a walkie-talkie, started to call someone for help, and peered back outside . . . but the man, the horses and the wagon had all vanished without a trace.

The dedicated, passionate team that work hard to maintain the Ukrainian Cultural Heritage Centre are proud to bring history to life each and every day. But many of them know that in this unique living museum, history never died.

# THE MAN FROM THE MIST

## *Algonquin Park, Ontario*

In the summer of 1980, Muskoka artist Doug Dunford spent two weeks in Algonquin Park, immersing himself in the natural beauty of the land. He was painting a new sign for the park, and he expected to capture the wildlife, the water and the trees. He never suspected he'd also capture a ghost.

Early one morning Doug walked down to the dock on Canoe Lake. A thick mist hung low over the water — it was eerily calm and quiet. For a long time he stood on the end of the dock with his camera hanging around his neck, enjoying the moment. But then the silence was broken. From somewhere within the mist, he heard the gentle splashing sound of a paddle breaking the surface of the water. A canoe suddenly became visible, steered by a lone man.

The two men made eye contact, and Doug was

overwhelmed by the sensation of a strange energy. He raised his camera to his eye and snapped a picture of the canoeist. And then, without a word, the stranger turned his head away from Doug and disappeared.

The brief experience was so quietly unnerving, even mystical, that Doug quickly began to doubt it had happened at all. It made no sense. Why was someone out canoeing alone in such thick mist so early in the morning? How had he disappeared right in front of Doug's eyes?

One thing Doug didn't question — even though he had no reason to believe it — was that the man had been Tom Thomson. Or more to the point, the man had been Thomson's ghost.

Tom Thomson was an artist famous for his sketches and paintings depicting the Canadian wilderness. He was also an outdoorsman who was skilled at fishing and canoeing. Although he died in 1917 before the establishment of the Group of Seven, he was friends with the artists who formed the group and is considered to be an unofficial member. For more than one hundred years, people have reported spotting Thomson quietly paddling across Canoe Lake, often on July 16, the anniversary of the day his body was found. It seems the artist hasn't been able to leave the lake behind.

Thomson had died eight days before his body was found floating in the lake. He had set out on a fishing trip in his canoe, and many suspect that his death wasn't an accident. His left temple was bruised and his left ankle was wrapped seventeen or eighteen times in fishing line. The blow to the head could be attributed to an accidental fall, perhaps, but the fishing line was harder to explain. Many people, such as Blodwen Davies, an official of the Saskatchewan Art Board who wrote a biography on Thomson, believe that he was struck on the head and that his body was tied to something heavy and dumped in one of the deepest parts of the lake. If this is true — if Tom Thomson was murdered — it would explain why his soul is unable to move on.

When Doug Dunford developed his photograph, he couldn't believe his eyes. Thomson's ghost had been captured on film. He felt drawn to paint the photograph; it was as if, as he says, the painting chose him. Once completed, Doug titled the watercolour *The Return of Tom Thomson*. He hung it in his art gallery six or seven years later. One day, a young man wandered into the gallery and was immediately drawn to the painting. He purchased it and left.

A year later Doug received a letter from the young man, explaining why he was compelled to purchase the painting. He had seen the exact same man in the exact same canoe on the same lake not long before and had been convinced that he had seen a ghost. He couldn't believe it when he spotted the painting, but he knew he couldn't live without it.

They are far from the only people who have seen Tom Thomson's ghost paddling across Canoe Lake. For example, in the summer of 1931, Mrs. Northway, who lived on the lake, her daughter and a guide were paddling on the lake at dusk when they saw another canoe approaching them. As they neared each other, the three saw that a solitary man was in the other canoe. Mrs. Northway raised her hand and called hello, but the man didn't respond. At that moment he vanished into thin air, canoe and all, and the only sound remaining on the lake was the call of a loon in the distance. Once the initial shock wore off, the party was convinced they'd spotted Thomson's ghost.

Every year on July 16, people gather on the shores of Canoe Lake, hoping to catch a glimpse of Tom Thomson, a testament to the impact his art has had on the country.

Tom Thomson in Algonquin Park, sometime between 1914 and 1916

# AFTERLIFE LIGHTS

## *Port Hardy, British Columbia*

The tires of Frank Chatain's car slowly came to a stop at the side of the road. He killed the ignition and sat and thought and grieved. It was early morning. The sun had not yet fully risen and the land was dim in the grey light. Alone, Frank stared through the windshield, his attention and his sorrow both focused solidly on one of the utility poles across the road from where he had parked.

It was 1986 and his beloved daughter, Tara, had died tragically several days before. She had borrowed a family car and allowed a friend to drive it. The friend lost control of the car on a corner and drove headfirst into the pole. Tara died instantly in the crash, just two weeks before her seventeenth birthday.

As Frank stared at the pole and grappled with his

sorrow, he noticed the street light bolted at its peak. The light was much dimmer than the others that lined the street.

*Probably damaged by the collision,* Frank thought.

The light went out and then, after a moment, came back on again.

An idea struck Frank. *Is that you, Tara?* he thought.

Immediately the light burned intensely bright, brighter than all of the other lights, and then returned to normal.

Frank was certain that his daughter was responsible for the changes in the light.

*Are you trying to communicate with me?*

. Once again, the light answered. It pulsed brightly a few times, as if desperate to get Tara's point across. After asking a few more questions and gauging the responses from the light, Frank had interpreted his daughter's code. If she made the light turn off, the answer to his question was *no.* If she made it turn brighter, the answer was *yes.* Armed with this knowledge, Frank asked a few more questions.

*Are you happy?*

The light burned bright, answering *yes.*

*Are you well?*

*Yes.*

Wherever she was, Tara was happy and well. While that didn't make up for the loss, it helped a little knowing she was all right. Frank drove back home.

Some time later Frank and his wife decided it was time to replace the car that had been destroyed in the accident. Unsurprisingly, the couple had no desire to go automobile shopping so soon after their daughter's tragic accident. The salesperson showed them all of the cars that fit their price range, but the Chatains weren't interested in any of them. Instead, they were drawn to a more expensive model — as if the car was choosing them rather than the other way around — and they decided to stretch their budget to buy it. Strangely, they had gone from dreading car shopping to being filled with happiness as they drove their new vehicle off the lot.

Before long, the couple were driving the new car on the highway between Campbell River and Port Hardy. Despite the fact that it was late, dark and raining, Frank was driving over the speed limit. Suddenly the headlights turned off. Frank couldn't see where he was headed, so he immediately slowed the car down. As he did, the headlights began to flash on and off, until he finally came to a complete stop and the headlights turned on again.

As they sat safely on the side of the road, Mrs. Chatain had a sudden realization. Her husband had told her what had happened the morning he had driven out to the scene of Tara's accident.

"Is that you, Tara?" she asked.

The headlights flashed off and on. *Yes.*

After the initial shock had worn off, Frank started driving again, but now at a much slower speed. Almost immediately the road turned sharply. Frank was certain he wouldn't have been able to make the turn safely in the rain at the speed he had been travelling before Tara had slowed him down.

The Chatains then knew why they had been drawn to

the car. For some reason, *Tara* had been drawn to the car.

For years after, as long as they had the car, Tara continued to flash the headlights whenever there were unseen threats ahead, such as another dangerous turn or a deer crossing the road. And Tara's personality shined through from time to time, such as one day when her parents drove to the airport to pick up her brother, who was returning home for a visit. She flashed the headlights in excitement all the way to the airport and most of the way home, stopping only when her brother finally acknowledged her presence and said hello to her.

Some ghosts have the ability to appear in human form, while others look like shadows and mist. Others still, like Tara, seem incapable of being seen by the living at all and need to come up with other methods to communicate. So the next time you see a light flicker inexplicably, you'll have to wonder if it's simply an electrical issue or if it's something more meaningful, perhaps more chilling. You'll have to wonder if the dead are speaking to you from beyond the grave.

# THE HAUNTED MANSION

## *Toronto, Ontario*

In 2003 a woman visited The Keg Mansion, a restaurant located in an historic Toronto building, for a relaxing meal with a friend. She told her friend that she'd been there twice before and had enjoyed the food, but she'd also been disturbed by a presence she had felt in the old, gothic-style building. The presence had felt strongest in the women's bathroom, so she'd asked the restaurant staff about it. She was told that Lillian Massey, a previous resident of the mansion, was one of the ghosts who haunted the building.

*One of the ghosts?* she had wondered. *How many ghosts are there?*

On this visit, the woman and her friend took a short self-guided tour of the building while they waited for their table to be ready. They were stopped when they reached the allegedly haunted bathroom. A little girl stood there.

"Are you talking," the girl said in a hushed tone, "about the ghost?"

"Yes," the woman said, seeing no reason to hide the truth.

The little girl stepped closer and lowered her voice further. She told them that a friend of hers always had a hard time entering that bathroom. She would feel eyes watching her.

On that disturbing note, the woman and her friend said goodbye to the little girl and went to see if their table was ready. Once they were seated and a third friend had joined them, the woman excused herself to use the bathroom.

As she pushed open the bathroom door, the woman instantly felt she was not alone. She glanced under every single stall. They all appeared to be empty. This didn't make her feel any better; in fact, it made her feel worse. She was suddenly overcome by panic, as she began to suspect she was being watched.

She hurried into the final stall and locked the door. Her knees were shaking from fear. Then she heard something move in the bathroom and approach the door to her stall.

The woman forced herself not to scream. She tried to calm down, tried to convince herself it wasn't really happening, tried to think of anything else, but then . . .

Then the lock slowly turned.

The door creaked open.

But there was no one there.

The woman stood petrified, feeling that at any moment she'd see the ghostly woman who had opened the door.

She broke free from the terror that had ensnared her and bolted out of the stall and the bathroom as if her life depended on it.

Once she had calmed down a little, she headed back to her table and her friends. But on her way, she passed the girl she had seen earlier. The woman started to tell her what had just happened, but the girl interrupted her.

"Did the lock pop open while you were in there?" she asked. "Because mine did."

This woman and girl aren't the only people to have experienced paranormal activity in the bathroom. Countless others have had nearly identical experiences, while some have also seen the toilet paper dispensers shake and have watched in horror as their personal items have floated in the air before being gently placed on the floor. And at least two people have seen the ghost with their own eyes.

The first was a woman who spotted feet in one of the stalls. A moment later the toilet flushed, the door opened . . . but there was no one in the stall.

The second was a woman named Mia who was dining in the restaurant for the first time. Mia went to the bathroom after her meal and felt like she was being watched the entire time. When Mia opened the door she saw a woman standing before her. She was wearing a beautiful, old-fashioned dress. The woman didn't move and didn't say a word. Mia said a quick "hello" that went unanswered. She had a weird feeling about the woman, so she hurried past her and down the stairs. On her way out of the restaurant, she asked the host about the woman.

"It's only four male servers tonight, no waitresses," the host said, adding, "and definitely no one in an old-fashioned dress."

The mansion was built in 1868 by Arthur McMaster and purchased in 1882 by one of the most prominent families in Toronto's history, the Masseys. Patriarch Hart Massey was an industrialist who helped found new buildings for the University of Toronto and the famous performing arts theatre that bears his name, Massey Hall. One of his grandsons, Vincent Massey, became Governor General of Canada in 1952, and another, Raymond Massey, was an Academy Award-nominated actor. Hart's only daughter, Lillian, an educator and philanthropist, took over the house and ran the family interests. She gave the mansion its first name, Euclid Hall. She loved the home so much that it appears she has decided to remain there forever, scaring scores of women who use the second floor bathroom.

As Lillian got older, her health began to fade. She was so ill that her time outside had to be severely limited, so an underground tunnel was constructed to connect the mansion with the Wellesley Hospital. Jenn Anthony, a former general manager at The Keg Mansion, reported that some people believe the spirits of those who died in the hospital still wander through the property, forever lost, confused and often in eternal pain.

Lillian Massey died in 1915. It's rumoured that one of the family's maids was so distraught by her passing that she hanged herself in the main foyer. Customers and staff have reported catching a glimpse of a body swinging from

*Alice Massey, Lillian's sister-in-law, poses outside Euclid Hall (now The Keg Mansion) with her son Lionel and an unidentified woman in 1922*

a length of rope. After a quick blink and a rub of the eyes, the maid's body disappears.

And there are plenty more ghosts in the mansion, including another mysterious woman spotted in the dining room. Melanie Elaraby went to the restaurant with her husband one Friday evening. She was overcome by a mix of excitement and anxiety as soon as she entered the building, and her heart began to flutter in her chest. Shortly after they were seated, Melanie felt a cold chill spread up her arm that covered her skin in goosebumps. She dismissed the feeling and placed her order, but it didn't stop there. It felt like cold fingers were caressing Melanie's hand. She kept thinking a fly might be crawling on her, but there was nothing there. When she moved her hand off the table, the feeling went away, but it came right back the moment she put her hand back on the table. And then the phantom touch moved to the back of her neck, and Melanie immediately saw a ghostly woman standing beside her — a woman only she could see. She was young, blond and had blue eyes set in a wide face. She wore her hair tied above her head and was dressed in a light blouse and a long skirt. The woman didn't speak, but Melanie got the feeling she was shy of her husband, who was still oblivious to the spectral presence. She remained beside Melanie for the rest of the meal, silently watching her eat. It's remarkable that Melanie had any appetite left at all.

Others regularly see and hear children playing on the stairs. Laura Dee has had two encounters with ghost children in The Keg Mansion. The first was when she was walking toward the bar and passed a dark-haired boy playing at the top of the stairs.

*Strange,* she thought, knowing that children weren't allowed in the bar at night. They aren't, but who would be able to kick out a ghost? When Laura looked again, the boy had vanished into thin air.

The second experience was in 2014. Laura walked upstairs to the bar with a friend, and as they passed the same spot where she had previously seen the dark-haired boy, they both stopped dead in their tracks. They could hear kids running up and down the stairs, laughing and yelling and making a racket. But there were no children there at all.

Spirits and steaks. Both can be found in abundance in The Keg Mansion.

# THE HAUNTING OF CHERRY HILL HOUSE

## Mississauga, Ontario

When asked by a local newspaper, the *Mississauga News,* to dispel the persistent rumours that Cherry Hill House was haunted, Ron Duquette was reluctant to agree. It's not that he was afraid of the building that's considered to be one of the most haunted houses in the city; he was a skeptic of the paranormal. Ghosts didn't exist, so what was the point in trying to prove there were none in Cherry Hill House? It would be a senseless endeavour, a waste of his time. When Ron finally agreed, he had no idea what horrors awaited him.

Built in 1822 by Joseph Silverthorn, a farmer, sawmill owner and militiaman who served during the War of 1812, Cherry Hill House was a large two-storey Georgian-style home. The name came from the cherry trees the family had planted along the driveway. Joseph lived in the house with his wife, Jane, and their twelve children. The Silverthorns were among the first settlers in the area, and the house, surrounded by woods that spanned seven hundred acres, is believed to be the oldest surviving structure in what is now the city of Mississauga. The Silverthorns owned the house until 1951.

For a time thereafter, an eccentric, reclusive old woman named Daisy Anne Lindsay occupied the house, and that's when the ghostly rumours surrounding the property really took hold. Among the local children, Daisy Anne became known as the Witch of Cherry Hill. The children who were brave enough to venture onto the property could often be spotted running and screaming back to safety as Daisy Anne flew out of the house in a threatening manner with a broom raised high above her head.

By the early 1970s, Daisy Anne had moved out and the house sat empty and abandoned. It had been significantly vandalized and many pieces of furniture had been stolen. However, several rope beds and an old spinning wheel remained, gathering dust and cobwebs as the years passed. The city wanted to build a new road straight through the property, but due to the house's historical significance, it was decided to move it more than 350 metres north to a new site, and that's when Ron Duquette was asked to prove that the rumours of it being haunted were false.

Those involved agreed that the best way to do so would be to hold a séance in one of the upper bedrooms, an area that had apparently been a hotbed of paranormal activity. It was an idea everyone present would live to regret.

It was a late night in early fall of 1973 and the woods surrounding Cherry Hill House were cold and dark. Ron Duquette and seven others, including a professional medium, walked up the front steps, over the creaky verandah, and through the front door. Once upstairs, they sat around an old table in the centre of the bedroom in complete darkness. Someone struck a match and lit a candle. The flame flickered and shadows danced on the walls. The medium asked everyone to hold hands and close their eyes. The group willingly did so and waited in stony silence broken only by the soft rustle of the wind blowing through the trees outside and the occasional groan of the house. As the medium called out to any spirits inhabiting the house, Ron heard footsteps slowly coming up the stairs, but no one appeared in the doorway.

A little while later, a young reporter from the newspaper unexpectedly began to shake in her seat. She writhed and kicked and spasmed violently for no apparent reason, moaning loudly as sweat poured down her flushed face. The rest of the group sat frozen in fear.

"My name is Hamish McKenzie," the young woman suddenly said, but her voice was not her own. Instead she spoke with the voice of an old Scottish man who sounded like he was in a great deal of pain.

Ron and the others listened in shock as the ghost of Hamish McKenzie communicated with them, using the poor young woman as a human loudspeaker. The reason he was in pain was because he had been injured in the Boer War. He had come to search for his relatives, the Silverthorns, and admitted that he was afraid to die.

No one had the heart — or the guts — to tell him he was already dead.

After five minutes speaking with McKenzie, the medium decided it would be best to end the conversation and the séance altogether. The young reporter was driven home and taken to her bed, where she remained for several days. She couldn't find the strength to rise and she had a pounding headache nearly the entire time. When she finally recovered and returned to her old self, she had no memory of the possession. Needless to say, Ron Duquette was no longer a skeptic.

In June the house was moved to its new location where it remains today, and the ghosts moved with it. Its notoriety continued to spread and many curiosity seekers attempted to sneak into the house, so the restoration team hired security guards to keep watch through the night. One of the guards, Ron Land, was sitting in his car when he saw a white shadow holding a long sword rise out of a mound of dirt. Ron cautiously exited his vehicle. His dog, Cindy, ran toward the spirit. But when the figure charged toward them, both Ron and Cindy turned and fled in terror. The next guard didn't last long either, as late one night he was confronted by a ghost riding a horse, both glowing brilliantly white in the moonlight. Like Ron Land, the guard fled the premises, never to return.

The house has been occupied more recently by a string of restaurants that can't seem to remain in business very long, leading some to believe the building is cursed. People have seen a number of spirits and had odd encounters. A little girl has been seen staring out of the upper windows

*Locals follow along as Cherry Hill House makes the journey north to its new location*

when the building is closed for the night. Lights dim on their own, glasses fall off tables, doors open and close, cold spots float through hallways and rooms, and reflections of ghosts have been caught in the mirrors.

Ashley Pacheco, a bartender who used to work in the building, would often place a bottle or a glass down on the bar only to find it somewhere else seconds later. Similarly, reporter Tina Robinson, who was having dinner in the restaurant while working on an article about the building's history, placed her fork on her left and her knife on her right. When she looked back down, the cutlery had been reversed. She asked the server if she had moved it, but the server looked at Tina as if she had lost her mind.

In 2005 an elderly woman had a lengthy and animated chat with someone without realizing she was speaking with a dead person. She was part of a large dining party, and when questioned by the others as to what she was doing, she replied, "I was having a conversation with the woman in the rocking chair by the fireplace." The rocking chair by the fireplace, however, was empty.

Margo Marshall, bar manager of one of the more recent restaurants, was closing up the downstairs pub. It was 2:30 a.m. and she was alone in the building. Suddenly, she heard a terrible crash on the floor above. She was too scared to go investigate, so she called the maître d' the next day to ask if anything had been out of the ordinary when he'd arrived that morning.

"A dining room table had been turned over and the glasses broken," he replied at once. One of the spirits, it would appear, didn't appreciate Margo's company so late at night.

People have wondered over the years who the ghosts are that refuse to leave Cherry Hill House, and most are quick to agree that they must be the original family who lived there. One of the most persistent theories is that one of Joseph and Jane Silverthorn's sons, George, is responsible for much of the ghostly goings-on, and there's a centuries-old mystery to support this belief.

George married Louise Leonard in June 1852, in the Dixie Union Chapel across the street from the family home.

A celebratory feast was held in Cherry Hill House following the ceremony, but the festivities were interrupted by a loud knock at the front door. George excused himself and stepped outside to speak with a man whom no one at the party knew. He didn't return. The woods around the house were searched and the depths of a nearby swamp were dragged to no avail. Neither George nor the mysterious man was ever seen again.

That's not to say that he had left the family home forever, for it is said that anytime George's disappearance is discussed within Cherry Hill House, the front door opens and closes all on its own.

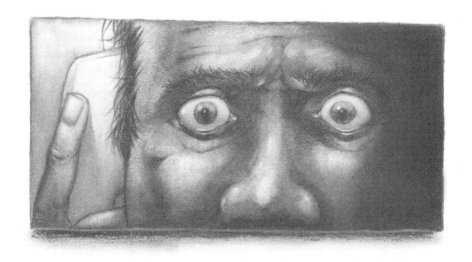

# TERROR ON THE THIRD FLOOR

## *Yellowknife, Northwest Territories*

It was nearly midnight when a man was startled out of his sleep. There had been a loud noise from the bathroom.

He was staying in the Quality Inn & Suites in downtown Yellowknife, and had hoped to get a good night's sleep, but that was proving to be impossible. Not only had something woken him up, but he had pulled a muscle in his rib cage earlier in the day and the pain was getting worse with every passing hour.

As he wondered what had caused the sound in the bathroom, he remembered that he had fallen asleep with the television on. Now it was turned off. Had he turned it off in a semi-conscious state and forgotten doing so? The room was too dark for his liking, so he grabbed the remote control from the bedside table and turned the TV back on.

Blue, flickering light from the screen cast a pallid glow over the room.

Slowly, still battling the pain of his pulled muscle, he got out of bed and poked his head into the bathroom. The tap was turned on and water was flowing into the sink. He might not have remembered turning off the TV but he was certain he hadn't left the tap on. He turned it off and then noticed a bar of hotel soap lying on the floor beside the bathtub. Had that been the cause of the sound that had woken him up? It seemed likely. As he wondered how the water had turned on and how the soap had been knocked to the floor, he suddenly felt like he wasn't alone. But then his pain intensified and he needed to lie back down in bed. He muted the TV but left it on.

Sleep didn't come. By 2 a.m. the pain was unbearable. Every small movement was excruciating. And then the feeling that he wasn't alone returned.

The man didn't dare look, but he was certain someone was standing at the foot of his bed. He closed his eyes tight and waited, but the "someone" didn't go away. Instead, it sat down on the bed beside his feet. His heart began to pound in his chest and his breath became heavy and laboured.

Despite the terror that had gripped him, the man managed to look at the foot of the bed. No one was there . . . but the TV had been turned off again and there was an indent in the mattress where he'd felt the presence. It looked like someone was sitting there, but the man saw no one there. When he moved his feet and sat up, the indent filled in as if the presence had stood up. He turned on the bedside lamp and looked back at the foot of the bed. The indent returned.

Overcome with fright and unsure what to do, he picked up the phone and dialed 0.

"Front desk," a woman on the other end of the line said. "May I help you?"

"Yes!" the man shouted frantically. "This is room 300. Is there any chance I can change my room to a lower level?"

"I'm sorry, but we are completely booked today. There aren't any more rooms."

The man begged her to double-check, so she put him on hold. Speaking to another person helped calm his nerves a little, but he was still feeling uneasy in the silence, so he turned the TV back on.

The woman returned and confirmed that the hotel was completely booked. She then asked, "Is everything okay with your room?"

The man briefly wondered where to begin. With his TV being turned off twice? With the tap turning on? With the soap being thrown to the floor? With the feeling of not being alone? Or with the feeling of someone sitting down at his feet and the indent of their invisible body?

"Everything is okay," he said reluctantly. It was easier than admitting the truth, which he knew would make him sound like he'd lost his mind. They wished each other a good night and hung up.

*Great, now what?* the man wondered. *Do I leave the hotel and book somewhere else?* He didn't want to spend another minute in the room, but after spending so much money on it he also didn't want to spend any more by checking into another hotel. Resigned to the fact that he had to stay there for the rest of the night, he left both the TV and the lamp on and tried to fall back asleep. Amazingly, he did.

But his sleep didn't last long. At 4:30 a.m. he was awoken by another sound. This time it wasn't the sound of soap falling in the bathroom. It was the sound of a woman screaming in one of the rooms next to his own.

"Who are you?" the woman screamed at the top of her lungs. "Get out!"

Once again feeling helpless and afraid, the man picked up the phone and dialed 0.

"Front desk. May I help you?"

"This is room 300 again," he said. "Someone is screaming down the hall in one of the rooms."

"Are you sure, sir? We didn't get any phone calls from your level."

"Yes! A lady shouted in distress, and—"

The staff member interrupted the man and asked him to hold. As he waited he realized the TV and lamp had been turned off, once again plunging the room into darkness. Before he could turn either back on, the woman returned on the line. She told him that other guests had just called to report the disturbance and that two security guards were on their way up to investigate.

The man hung up and turned on the TV and the lamp. He didn't even bother trying to fall back asleep. Instead, he lay awake as he waited for the sun to rise, bringing an end to the horrible night.

Time passed slowly, but finally it was time to check out.

He packed up and wheeled his suitcase down the hall. As he passed two housekeepers he caught a snippet of their conversation.

". . . no one was in the room but people called downstairs . . ."

If no one had been in the room, why had the front desk staff said the entire hotel was booked?

The feeling of someone sitting down on his bed occupied his thoughts as he waited for the elevator, and he was so engrossed that the *ding* indicating it had reached the third floor startled him.

When he arrived at the main floor, the woman at the front desk greeted him. He could tell by her voice that it wasn't the same person he had spoken with twice during the night.

"Did you like your room?" she asked brightly, a wide smile on her face.

"To be honest, no," the man said. He was tired, sore, and more than a little upset thanks to the night's events, and he could no longer keep his thoughts to himself even if it *did* make him sound like he'd lost his mind. He told her about all the odd things that had happened overnight.

The woman stared at him with an open mouth and wide eyes. But instead of thinking he was crazy, she believed him.

"Sir, you're not the first person to mention that," she said. She leaned in a little closer and admitted that a couple who had recently stayed in the same room had claimed they had seen a man appear in the middle of the night. He wore old-fashioned clothing and a miner's hat.

Interestingly, the Quality Inn & Suites was originally an independent hotel called the Yellowknife Inn. It was opened in the 1940s and its most popular feature among locals was the main floor diner called the Miner's Mess.

The man checked out, wishing he could leave his memories behind like a forgotten piece of luggage. Unsurprisingly, this proved as difficult to do as falling asleep in a haunted hotel room, and he carries those memories with him to this day.

# BESSIE'S MISSING BODY

## *Carcross, Yukon*

Archie Lang, manager of the Caribou Hotel, felt like someone was watching him. It was the middle of the night and he had been asleep in one of the upper floor guest rooms when he had been awoken suddenly — not by a sound or a touch, but by a sickening feeling in the gut.

As he opened his eyes, he discovered he truly wasn't alone. There was a woman in the doorway staring back at him. When she saw that Archie had spotted her, she sped to the foot of his bed.

Archie sat up in shock and couldn't figure out why Agnes Johns, the hotel's chambermaid, had snuck into his room in the dead of night.

"Agnes?" he said. "What are you doing here?"

Agnes didn't answer. Agnes didn't move. Agnes, Archie

quickly realized, wasn't actually Agnes. The woman in his room was someone else. Someone he didn't know.

Archie bolted out of bed. This seemed to startle the woman, and she turned and raced out of the room. Desperate to know who she was and what she was doing, Archie chased her to the top of the stairs. She raced down, her feet not making a sound on the old, creaky steps. He reached the bottom in a flash, but the woman had disappeared.

Confused and a little uneasy, Archie went back to bed. The next morning, as he was preparing the restaurant for the day, his friend Johnny entered the hotel. Archie told him about the mysterious woman who had visited him in the night, describing what she looked like and how oddly she had acted.

After a moment of silence, Johnny said with certainty, "You just described Mrs. Gideon."

The macabre reality of Johnny's statement took a minute to sink in. Bessie Gideon was one of the previous owners of the hotel. She had died nearly forty years earlier, in 1933.

After the Klondike Gold Rush exploded in 1896, many prospectors travelling from Alaska into Yukon stopped to rest in the town of Caribou Crossing before continuing on to Dawson City. Caribou Crossing was a key hub for mail delivery and telegraph communications, and from 1898 served as a station for the White Pass and Yukon Railway. The town's name was shortened to Carcross so that it wouldn't be confused with similarly named towns in western Canada and Alaska. One of the oldest remaining structures in Yukon, the Caribou Hotel was built in Bennett, British Columbia, in 1898. As Carcross grew, Bennett became a ghost town. In 1901 the original owner, W. H. Anderson, floated the hotel up Lake Bennett to Carcross and renamed it the Anderson Hotel.

Two years later, Anderson sold the hotel to "Dawson" Charlie, one of the first two men to discover gold near Dawson City, for a reported $9,000. Charlie remodelled the hotel and changed the name back. He fell from a bridge and died in 1908. And that's when Bessie Gideon entered the picture, a picture she has refused to leave.

She and her husband Edwin leased the hotel from Charlie's estate, unaware that tragedy was just around the corner. A fire broke out in 1909 and destroyed the hotel. Faced with the choice to cut their losses and move on or rebuild, the Gideons chose the latter option. The new hotel opened in 1910.

Bessie died in the hotel just days before Halloween in 1933, which was coincidentally eight years to the day after her husband had died. She was buried beside him in the Carcross Cemetery . . . or so everyone thought. But a 1998 cemetery survey was unable to locate her grave, leading people to wonder what became of Bessie's body. And if she wasn't buried with her husband as per her wish, did that explain why her spirit has been so restless and troublesome?

During World War II, when the U.S. Army had temporarily taken over the hotel, Bessie repeatedly turned on an old army cooking stove late at night. More recently, Bessie has been known to knock on people's doors and disappear. Her footsteps have been heard creaking across the upper floors at all hours. She has turned on lights even when the electricity was completely shut off for renovations. Multiple people have even reported that she has added bubbles to their baths.

Bessie is often seen staring out of the second and third floor windows of the hotel, watching people pass by on the street. Those who see her ghost sometimes also see a second ghost perched on her shoulder: Polly, Bessie's beloved parrot.

Polly came to the Caribou Hotel in 1918, when Captain James Alexander asked Bessie to look after his pet while he and his wife sailed south for the winter. Bessie agreed, but Captain Alexander didn't return. The *Princess Sophia*, the ship he had sailed on, ran aground on Vanderbilt Reef. There were no survivors. Polly remained in the hotel and long outlived Bessie, dying in 1972 at the ripe old age of 126. During his life he became famous for singing opera, drinking whiskey, biting people's fingers and shocking guests by squawking bad words at inappropriate times. Although Bessie's grave can't be found in the Carcross Cemetery, Polly's grave is situated there in a place of honour with a beautiful bronze marker. An elaborate funeral, with dignitaries attending from Whitehorse and beyond, followed the parrot's death.

In 2015 Canada Post unveiled a special stamp that portrays Bessie looming large above her beloved hotel — dressed in her finest clothes, her hair beautifully styled atop her skull. In September of that year, shortly after the stamp's unveiling, owner Anne Morgan welcomed

Bessie's great-grandniece, Janette, to visit. The hotel was under renovation, but Anne offered to give Janette a private tour. She wanted to show Janette the owner's suite on the second floor, the room that had been occupied by Bessie long ago, but a board screwed to the wall blocked the unfinished

*The ghost of Bessie Gideon with the Caribou Hotel on a 2015 postage stamp*

staircase. Anne went to retrieve an electric drill so that they could go upstairs.

From the next room, Anne heard Janette call loudly up the stairs. She was calling Bessie's spirit, explaining who she was and how they were related.

For a moment, silence, and then — *Bang! Bang!*

Bessie had knocked twice on the wall, loud as a drum, on the second floor.

Anne took a moment to compose herself and then returned to Janette. Bessie's distant relative was shaking and pale. The tour ended then and there, but Bessie's haunting of the hotel hasn't, and it likely never will.

# THE ASP

## Ottawa, Ontario

The fourth floor attic of Lisgar Collegiate Institute, Ottawa's oldest secondary school, is legendary among the student body. Kids regularly dare each other to sneak up to it. Few have the guts. Those who do are sometimes locked in the attic by their friends. And what they see up there is often too terrifying to talk about.

There was a janitor in the early 1940s who had a fearsome reputation. Students nicknamed him The Asp, after the highly venomous snake that was the symbol of royalty in ancient Egypt and used as a method of execution in ancient times. Step out of line, leave behind a mess, or do something you shouldn't have done, and The Asp would nearly always catch you in the act. He had the uncanny ability to turn a corner or appear out of the shadows at precisely the worst moments, and he wasn't shy to speak his mind and chastise students. But he was still a valued member of the janitorial team, and was known to be a hard worker who took pride in fixing problems quickly and skillfully. That didn't endear him to the students, however, who resented him for ruining their fun more times than not. To the students, The Asp was anti-social, old and cranky. He probably wasn't too happy the fateful day he was sent out onto the roof to clear a buildup of snow and ice.

Earlier that day, Lisgar's head girl had been walking outside alone. As she passed beneath the round attic window, a slab of heavy ice broke free from the roof and struck her, killing her instantly. Reeling from the shock of the tragedy, school officials sent all of the janitors out to clear the remaining snow off the roof.

The Asp stepped onto the roof through a door at one end of the attic. He didn't make it much farther than that. The roof was steeply sloped and slick with ice. He lost his footing, slipped, and fell to his death below, landing very close to the same spot where the girl had died earlier.

The first reports of hauntings soon followed, unsurprising given the tragic and gruesome nature of the back-to-back deaths. Students looked up to catch a glimpse of the girl in the fourth floor window, staring at the world below. It was believed that she was keeping a watchful eye in an attempt to protect others from the same fate. But despite her good intentions, the sight of the young ghost looking down at people from the attic was chilling.

The surviving janitors complained that the temperature

dropped considerably when passing the attic door to the roof, even in the summer when the rest of the school was stiflingly hot. And as they went about their work in the attic, they felt like they were constantly being watched by someone who wasn't physically there. Over time the janitors learned to avoid the fourth floor late at night, but even those who work on the third floor after the school has closed for the day hear weird, inexplicable sounds coming from the floor above.

Another odd late-night phenomenon is the sight of balls of light — also known as ghost orbs — floating in the attic. This has been seen by people who live in the area as well as tourists taking part in Ottawa's Haunted Walk; Lisgar Collegiate Institute is a key stop on the tour.

In the 1970s the school underwent a large renovation, and an inspector made a startling discovery in the attic. Several electrical fires had started within the walls over the years, but somehow, defying any reasonable explanation, they had all gone out on their own. Whispers started to spread, wondering if The Asp — the janitor who was so dedicated to fixing problems when he wasn't busting misbehaving students — had saved the school from burning down.

And those students who were dared to explore the fourth floor only to be locked in by their friends? While many have been too scared to share what they saw, some have reported seeing a dark shadow walk beside them or a wispy figure drifting across the floor.

Today the area in the courtyard beneath the sloped roof is fenced off during the winter to prevent anyone else from being injured, and the attic is only used for storage. Even if one of the two ghosts who haunt the floor don't make an appearance, it's a creepy place filled with old uniforms, discarded laboratory equipment and a human skeleton from the biology lab, all covered in thick strands of cobwebs and dust. And that's exactly how the school spirits like it.

Lisgar Collegiate Institute, built in 1874

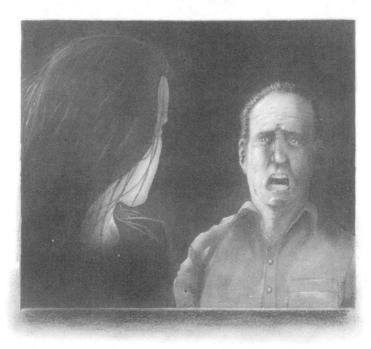

# SPIRIT CLUB

## *Montreal, Quebec*

A young woman had heard the rumours about the night-club at 1234 Rue de la Montagne, and she needed to see for herself if they were true. Word on the street was that it used to be a mortuary, and that evil spirits dwelled in the basement, the main floor and the attic. Curious, she broke off from the friends she'd arrived with and asked a waiter if she could go up to the attic, just for a moment or two.

"Absolutely not," he said. "The attic is off limits."

His refusal did nothing but stoke the fires of her curiosity. Before she had been curious; now she was obsessed. As soon as he turned his back and could no longer see her, she snuck up the stairs into the attic.

Moments later the patrons below heard a terrible scream that was loud enough to cut through the deep bass of the dance music. Since they were on the main level of the club, they didn't see what happened next. But the bouncers outside at the front door saw it all.

The woman went through the attic window and landed amid a shower of broken glass on the balcony. Screaming hysterically, she got to her feet and, without pause, threw herself off the balcony. Fortunately, one of the bouncers was able to catch her, possibly saving her life. She kicked and screamed and tried to break free, so he dragged her into the club to stop the scene from getting worse. He also didn't want her to hurt anyone, including herself, more than she already had.

Laura, a bartender who worked at the club in 2005, when the shocking incident occurred, was there when the woman was brought inside. The woman continued to scream at the top of her lungs non-stop for what felt like an eternity. Her words were gibberish and nonsensical, but what was very clear was that she had seen something truly terrifying, something that made her snap and nearly lose her mind. Finally the police and paramedics arrived. With a great deal of effort, they managed to get her onto a stretcher and wheel her to an ambulance, but she didn't stop screaming for a second. Laura began to wonder if the poor woman had been possessed.

The rumours the woman had heard were absolutely true; the nightclub used to be a mortuary and it is, by many accounts, haunted. Built in 1859 as a private residence that was first owned by David R. Wood, a wealthy businessman, and then by Sir Alexander Tilloch Galt, a politician and father of Canadian Confederation, the grand

*1234 Rue de la Montagne in 1899*

building was converted in 1902 into the Joseph C. Wray & Bros. Funeral Home. It served this purpose until 1970 when the company moved to a new location, and 1234 Rue de la Montagne sat abandoned for eight years before being purchased and converted once more, this time into a high-end nightclub. It has changed management and names many times over the years, causing people to wonder if each owner has been scared off the premises by the spirits who refuse to leave after the bar closes.

The worst of the ghosts — at least in physical appearance — is a woman who has been seen in the bar area on the first floor. Late one night during renovations in the 1970s, construction workers saw a large ball of light — a ghost orb — float through the air toward them. They called the owner to complain, admitting they were too scared to continue working in the building at night, but he laughed it off and dismissed their concerns. A few other people had mentioned to him that the building was haunted, but he hadn't seen anything himself and didn't believe any of the stories he'd heard. All the same, his curiosity was piqued, so he visited the club late one night, partly to see how the renovations were progressing but mostly to prove that nothing unusual was going on.

The door was locked and all of the workers had gone home by the time he arrived. The building was completely empty, or so he thought. There was a woman in a black dress standing by the bar with her back to him. He approached cautiously, not wanting to startle her and also a little concerned that she had gotten in. He took a seat at the bar beside her and opened his mouth to ask her if she needed any help, but she turned around before he uttered a word. When she faced him, he nearly fell to the floor.

The woman in the black dress didn't have a face. It looked like her skin had been removed. Horrified and revolted by the gruesome creatures standing before him, he turned and ran out of the building as fast as he could. And he never returned, opting to sell the club to someone else instead of seeing the renovations through to completion. It's fitting that the name of the first club to open its doors was Club l'Esprit, which means Spirit Club in English.

Monica Wizinski, who worked at the club when it was called World Beat Complex, once heard an odd sound on the main floor before it had opened to the public. When she entered the room alone to investigate, she saw a large ball of blue light floating in mid-air, just as the construction workers had seen years before. She watched it for a moment, completely mesmerized, before it shot toward her and entered her body through her outstretched hand. She described the feeling of the light passing through her as crazy and overwhelming, and as soon as it shot back out of her, she was certain that the light had been a ghost. Luckily the spirit didn't do anything worse to her. Not everyone who has come into contact with one of the ghosts can say the same.

One night a young patron was washing her hands in the downstairs bathroom when another woman approached her quickly from behind. The new woman was deathly pale and had large black circles under her eyes, but those weren't the two physical characteristics that stood out the most. Instead, the young patron was most taken by — and terrified of — the thick red scars on her chest in a Y pattern and the fact that she was transparent. She thought it looked like the ghost had had an autopsy performed on her body. Before she had another thought, however, the ghost grabbed her around the neck and squeezed. The patron struggled to break free but was unable to do so. As they struggled the ghost disappeared and reappeared a few times. But even when she couldn't be seen she could still be felt, her invisible fingers maintaining their vise-like grip around the patron's neck. Finally, just as the patron thought she might pass out, the ghost let her go and disappeared once and for all.

During a taping of a French television show called *Rencontres Paranormales* in 2010, popular DJ and owner at the time MC Mario invited a team of paranormal investigators into the club. He had seen doors slam and heard the voice of a little girl singing, and wanted some answers. The team conducted a séance in the basement, sitting around a table with their palms flat on the surface. After asking a series of questions of the spirits, one finally answered by rocking the table. They quickly established that it was Sir Alexander Tilloch Galt's first wife. She had spent a good deal of her afterlife annoyed by the loud music because it bothered one of her daughters, another spirit who had remained in the building after death. The group asked if Mrs. Galt would agree to leave the living in peace if MC Mario played a piece of music composed by Mozart at the beginning of each evening. The ghost agreed.

MC Mario maintained his end of the deal, and no further paranormal activity was reported until he sold the building in 2013. Once the new club opened its doors and stopped MC Mario's opening ritual, the hauntings returned.

But what did the young woman who jumped out of the attic in 2005 see up there that caused her delirium? It's a question that has plagued many people to this day, including others who have entered the attic alone, whether on purpose or by accident. One night not too long after the woman had been sped away in an ambulance, three staff members dared each other to go see the empty room for themselves. After waiting for a few tense minutes in silence, they spotted a shadow floating by the wall. They didn't stick around to get a better look. They returned the way they had come — and who could blame them?

Some people come to dance their blues away. Others come to dance . . . and leave three shades paler than when they'd arrived.

# I'M INNOCENT

## St. Andrews, New Brunswick

In the fall of 1878, Thomas Dowd and Eliza Ann Ward were taken to the jail in St. Andrews and locked in separate cells. The jail had a horrible reputation. It had been purposely designed in 1832 to be as uncomfortable and inhospitable as possible. Each cell was cramped, dark, poorly ventilated and unheated in the winter — in fact, prisoners needed to be let out of their cells on the coldest days so that they wouldn't freeze to death.

Thomas and Eliza were charged with the axe murder of her husband, and their trial was held in the courthouse next door. Thomas maintained his innocence throughout the entire trial, but both he and Eliza were found guilty of the heinous crime. Thomas was sentenced to death by hanging, but Eliza was pregnant so she was sentenced to seven years' imprisonment. Unaware that Eliza was to be spared the hangman's noose, Thomas eventually confessed that he alone had killed her husband in order to spare her life.

On January 14, 1879, Thomas Dowd was hanged. Eliza was permitted to watch through a window in the jail. The execution brought her to tears.

It wasn't long before the jail became even more bleak and forbidding than it had been before. The guards heard strange sounds at night. One saw a mysterious beam of light appear on the wall of Thomas's cell and float in an odd, fluid pattern. Another couldn't believe his eyes as he watched a ghostly hand scratch a shaky proclamation on the wall:

*I'm innocent*

Eliza served her seven-year sentence but died shortly after she was released. She left behind a letter that was discovered by the authorities. In it, she confessed that she had been the only person responsible for the murder of her husband. As Thomas had claimed — both during the trial and in the afterlife — he was innocent.

There is another ghost who haunts the Old Gaol and Charlotte County Courthouse, as they're known today. He is also named Thomas, but unlike Thomas Dowd, this ghost is neither innocent nor docile.

Thomas Hutchings was an English sergeant in the Royal Air Force stationed at Pennfield Ridge, and was convicted of murdering a local girl in 1942. Like Thomas Dowd, Thomas Hutchings was hanged for his crime at the jail, and his ghost is most often seen in the courthouse next door, where he was sentenced. These days, tour guides lead people through both buildings while Hutchings does his best to make them flee.

One morning a tour guide arrived early to make sure everything was in order for the day. While checking on the main area of the courthouse, she heard a loud banging noise coming from the bathroom. But the noise stopped as abruptly as it had begun, so she went about her business and tried to forget all about it. When the banging started up again, she rushed to the bathroom to investigate. It was completely empty. It's believed Thomas Hutchings was venting some of the anger that he had saved up for decades.

Later that day, once a group of people had assembled in the courthouse, the guide began the tour. But some of the participants couldn't see it through to the end. The first was a man who lagged behind the others and remained in the courtroom as the group moved to a different area. Thomas Hutchings suddenly appeared sitting in the defendant's chair, glaring at the man with a look of pure hatred. The man was so scared that he abandoned the tour and ran outside. The second was a woman who stopped to admire some old photos on the wall. As she looked at one in particular, a man's handprint suddenly formed in the red velvet that framed the picture. She also couldn't stand to be in the courthouse any longer and ran outside. The third and final person who had a supernatural encounter during that same tour was an elderly man who spent a little time examining a collection of old city maps in one of the back rooms. First he heard the sound of footsteps coming from above, and then Hutchings appeared, standing in the corner of the room, his face twisted in anger. The old man ran from the courthouse as fast as he could and found the other two people a safe distance from the building. They shared the stories of what had happened to each of them and couldn't believe that they all had had similar experiences. One thing was clear: Hutchings didn't appreciate their presence. Elaine Bruff, who used to lead Heritage Discovery Tours in St. Andrews, admitted that when people would discuss Thomas Hutchings within the courthouse, bad things would often happen.

Tour guide Felicity Cooper and Charlotte County Archives archivist and manager Janice Fairney claim that people have seen coat hangers move on their own and blinds open and close in the judge's chamber. Women's necklaces have been lifted off their necks by invisible hands. Cooper says that she regularly feels someone touching her back as she shares stories from the courthouse's history.

As scary as Thomas Hutchings's activity in the courthouse can be, what he does in the jail is far, far worse. In 2009, filmmaker Paul Kimball spent some time with his friend Holly in Hutchings's cell late one Saturday night. The Old Gaol has occasionally allowed guests and tour participants to be locked in the old, dank cells to see if they're visited by the ghost. But Paul was a self-proclaimed skeptic and didn't believe in spirits from beyond the grave. He was sure Hutchings wouldn't be able to do anything to him, so there was no reason to be concerned. He couldn't have been more wrong.

After a little time had passed, Paul began to joke

around and challenged Hutchings to appear in the dark jail cell. Nothing happened. The seconds ticked by. He and Holly fell silent. And that's when things took a turn for the worse. Paul began to feel a cold sensation around his neck. It didn't feel normal at all. It felt like the cold was wrapping around his throat.

Just as he was going to tell Holly about the odd feeling, she cried out. She had seen a shadowy figure float through the cell. Despite the fright they'd both had, they tried to remain in the cell. But seven minutes later, Paul once again felt the cold wrap around his neck. That was enough, and they went out into the hallway.

Once they had told their tour guide what had happened, she smiled mischievously. She told them that she hadn't said anything before because she didn't want to influence their experience, but many people have reported that they have seen shadows in Hutchings's cell and felt ice-cold hands try to choke them.

The Charlotte County Jail

There's a sign on one of the Old Gaol's outer doors that reads,

*Thomas likes to hold the door "shut!"*

*Please push hard to open and come in!*

*Thank you*

The sign doesn't make it clear which Thomas, Dowd or Hutchings, which raises two chilling questions: Is it Dowd who is trying to protect people by keeping them out? Or Hutchings who is trying to terrorize people by keeping them trapped within?

# GHOST TOWN

## Chance Cove Provincial Park, Newfoundland and Labrador

There used to be a tiny village named Chance Cove, in what is now a provincial park, on the southern shore of the Avalon Peninsula. All that remains of it are ruins, the nightly disembodied wails of people dying and ghosts.

Chance Cove was a small fishing settlement of approximately fifty people in the late 1800s, nearly completely cut off from the outside world — and that's exactly how its residents liked it. Their privacy was very important to them and allowed them to live less than savoury lives. It allowed them to get away with murder.

Only one person, a delivery man from a distant community, was regularly welcomed to Chance Cove, but more out of necessity than friendship. For many years he travelled the path through the woods by horse and buggy, bringing food and supplies to Chance Cove every few days.

As the man rode into town one day, he was surprised that no one welcomed him. The streets were empty. All was quiet. Although it struck him as odd — the townsfolk always rushed out to greet him and look over his latest shipment — he shrugged it off and figured that everyone must be in their homes or down by the shore. He carried on to the spot where he always unloaded his wares, but still no one came out to help him with the cargo.

Beginning to grow more than a little uneasy, the man approached the nearest house. He knocked on the door. No one answered. He peered in a window. He couldn't see a soul. He called out loudly. No response. He checked every single house in Chance Cove — it didn't take long — and even let himself into a few of them. But there wasn't a single person to be found; no man, woman or child.

Now scared, the man noticed laundry left drying on clotheslines, buckets of water that had been tipped over, and tools scattered all over the place. Having heard rumours over the years that Chance Cove was haunted, he began to believe that the spirits who were said to appear out of the ocean after nightfall had stormed the town, and that everyone had fled in terror. The delivery man raced back to his horse and rode out of Chance Cove as quickly as possible, never to return.

The townsfolk, it was later discovered, had indeed abandoned Chance Cove in a mass evacuation. They walked to Trepassey and boarded a ship bound for America. They settled in Maynard, Massachusetts, and tried to begin their lives anew. But the memories of what had happened in Chance Cove haunted them all to their dying days. They couldn't talk about it with anyone who hadn't been there, and took the details of the event that drove them away from their home to their graves. It seemed plain to everyone who was familiar with the town that something supernatural had happened that night.

People trace the origin of the town's haunted history back to 1863, the year of the tragic wreck of the *Anglo Saxon*. The *Anglo Saxon* was a three-masted steamship used to bring immigrants from Great Britain to Canada. It departed Liverpool, England, on April 16 for Quebec City.

The ship didn't arrive at its destination. On April 27 a thick fog enshrouded the coast of Newfoundland, and the ship struck the shore near Clam Cove, roughly fifteen minutes south of Chance Cove by foot. Chief engineer William McMaster and other crew members attempted to get all 444 people off the ship by rigging a studding sail boom from the ship's rail to a nearby rock. They succeeded in getting 97 to safety, but everyone else drowned when the ship broke apart and was washed away in the waves. More than 100 bodies washed ashore and were buried on the banks, while the rest were lost forever.

At the time of the wreck, Chance Cove was uninhabited, but soon after a few families settled in the area. They made their living fishing, growing potatoes and turnips, and building boats. But whispers spread among some outlying communities that the people of Chance Cove were not to be trusted. Ships continued to run aground on the southeastern shore of Newfoundland with alarming frequency, and some believed the townsfolk were responsible. It was said they lit large fires on the cliffs and beaches, confusing sailors about how to navigate around the coastline. When the ships ran aground, the townsfolk stormed them and murdered everyone on board. They then took everything of value and allowed the ocean to consume the rest, including the dead.

But the dead didn't stay in their watery graves. Legend has it that the ghosts of the drowned surfaced every night to torment the people of Chance Cove. And the ghostly activity tends to be worse every year on April 27, the anniversary of the wreck of the *Anglo Saxon*. Spectral wails and cries erupt on the shore, but when the living run to investigate, believing another ship to have been wrecked, there is never anyone to be found.

A writer named John W. White visited Chance Cove after it had been abandoned and described what he had witnessed in an 1898 article for the *Newfoundland Quarterly*. He ruled out poverty and any other rational explanation for the mass exodus, since the homes were left in such pristine condition and fully furnished. The only explanation he could think of was that the ghosts — "inhabitants of the other world," he called them — had driven the townsfolk away. Their heart-rending screams from the shore and their nightly appearances on the streets of the town must have grown too awful to live with.

During the summer of the same year that White wrote about the town, a group of northern fishermen sailing in schooners discovered Chance Cove. They decided to stay in the houses for the season, setting off to fish early each morning. But like the original inhabitants, the fishermen soon found the town to be too frightening. They set fire to the buildings before leaving, hoping to eradicate the evil that dwelled there.

It didn't work. Chance Cove was turned into a provincial park in the early 1970s, and all that remains of the buildings are foundations, cellars, and a graveyard nearly completely swallowed by the woods. Residents of the Southern Shore continue to report activity whenever they venture too close to Chance Cove. They hear the ringing of ships' bells and the cries of people drowning. Some see strangers walk out of the night mist before disappearing. The activity continues to be most prevalent on April 27.

If you visit Chance Cove, chances are very good you won't be able to last through the night.

# DOWN IN THE DEPTHS

## *Bell Island, Newfoundland and Labrador*

On a beautiful Sunday afternoon in 1966, a group of Bell Island locals were completely unprepared for the sight that was about to confront them. They saw a procession of men in miner's gear coming from the mines as if their shift had just ended. But that didn't make sense. The mines didn't operate on Sundays, and all of the men who worked there were at home resting.

The miners walked slowly past as the people stared at them in silence. Then, without a word, the line of men vanished into thin air. That's when the group realized that the men were miners who had died on the job.

Starting in 1895, when iron mining began on Bell Island, the mines claimed the lives of at least 106 men. Miners etched white crosses into the tunnel walls as a grim reminder of the fallen. But the fallen have their own way to remind the living of the many tragedies that have taken place over the years.

In the 1940s, the mining company began to use a more powerful type of dynamite. One day two men set a charge that resulted in a blast twice as large as they had predicted. They hadn't been a safe enough distance away, and one of the men was killed. It was a miracle his partner survived.

After recuperating, the survivor returned to work in the mines and was even considering returning to the explosives crew despite what he had lived through, but then he saw something that changed his mind forever. His deceased co-worker appeared in the shaft before him, his face bloody and scarred. The ghost reached out his hand and then vanished. The incident left the miner so rattled that he never touched explosives again.

Other miners saw the same ghost for many years after. He'd often be spotted standing near the area where he'd lost his life. When approached he always turned and passed straight through the rocky wall.

Once the ghost made a rare trip out of the mines and into the light of day. His wife had been overwhelmed by grief and spent most afternoons standing at the exit to the shafts, watching the men stream past on their way to their homes, forever hoping — no matter how unlikely it seemed — to catch one final glimpse of her husband. She got her wish, but not how she'd imagined. Once the other miners had cleared out, she spotted one last man standing a short distance away. Although his back was turned to her, she knew right away that it was her husband; she could tell by his clothes and by his stance. Before she stopped to consider that what she was seeing wasn't possible, she raced to his side and called his name. He turned around slowly, and she gazed at him. Just as others had reported, his face was covered in blood.

*Men working at the mine in Wabana, Bell Island*

Another ghost that has been seen by many is that of an eighteen-year-old man. The spirit, easily mistaken for a living person, often joins miners at the beginning of their shifts. One miner recalls the morning that the young man walked beside him and struck up a conversation, excitedly sharing that it was his first day on the job. A moment later the older miner watched in shock as the younger man disappeared.

The confused and frightened miner told a co-worker what had happened, and that man then shared a story of his own.

Years before, a young man had been put on scraping duty on his first day in the mines, tasked with removing loose stones from recently dug sections of the mine. A falling rock struck him on the head, but he was wearing a helmet, so he figured he was okay. Eager to make a good impression on his first day, he didn't tell anyone and carried on working. Later he became very dizzy and collapsed. Another miner ran to his aid, but it was too late; shortly thereafter the young man died from the head injury. In the years that followed, many people saw the ghost of the young man who had died on his first day of work, and he always disappeared before entering the tunnel where the accident occurred. He appeared so frequently that, according to Bell Island historian Henry Crane, #2 Mine needed to be shut down permanently.

Although all of the mines have been closed for many years, the ghosts continue to haunt the island. In fact, since Tourism Bell Island began offering tours of the mines, ghostly encounters have increased.

Strange noises come from deep within the shafts, such as the clangs and bangs of picks and shovels striking rocks, voices talking and calling to one another, and an odd hissing sound that no one can explain. People are often touched on the shoulder or back by invisible hands, and cold spots glide through the darkness.

In 2015 Melissa McCall was touring the mines with her family. As they were about to enter, the guide told the group that back when the mines were still in operation, women weren't allowed to enter — it was believed to be bad luck. Melissa was in the back of the group and stayed behind to take a picture as the others moved along. "Girls aren't allowed in this area," she said in a mocking tone, and laughed at how ridiculous that was. But when she looked through her photos later in the evening, she couldn't believe what she found. In the picture she'd taken, there was a man staring at her from out of the darkness — a man who had definitely not been there before.

In 2016 a woman named Ruthann was on a tour with her fiancé and also saw a ghost, but instead of seeing him in a picture she saw him in the flesh, so to speak. The guide led the group around a corner and Ruthann spotted a tunnel with a sign that said it was a restricted area. The tunnel was pitch black, but Ruthann could see a light about three metres away. At first she assumed it was a permanent fixture, but then it began to bob up and down. It wasn't a light on the wall or ceiling; it was a light on a miner's helmet. Ruthann looked a little harder and could make out the dark outline of a man wearing the helmet, his face featureless and black. When she told the guide what she had seen, the guide calmly replied, "You just witnessed a ghost."

Ruthann wasn't convinced. "It could be just one of the other people," she said, hoping that was true.

"Definitely not," the guide said flatly. "No one — and I mean no one — is allowed down that way."

No one but the ghosts, that is.

# AND THE GHOSTS PLAYED ON

## Vancouver, British Columbia

Bill Allman, house manager at the Vogue Theatre, was locking up the building alone late one summer night in 1994. He made his way through various areas of the theatre — the stage, the projection booth, the dressing rooms — and eventually headed down to the basement. Bill walked from room to room, satisfied that each was empty before moving to the next, but then he stopped in the carpentry room. He was suddenly overwhelmed by the gut-churning sense that someone was right behind him. He spun around and was horrified to find his feeling had been correct. A three-dimensional shadow floated past the door. It was grey, translucent and held a human form. He bolted into the hall, but the shadow person was gone. Bill claims he set a speed record for exiting the theatre after the encounter. Unfortunately, it wouldn't be the last time he'd come across the shadowy ghost.

A month or two later, Bill was walking up the stairs to the stage. A drum kit was set up for a Beatles tribute band, but the musicians weren't on stage yet. All the same, Bill heard someone begin to play a basic drum beat: one kick on the bass drum followed by one hit on the snare, repeated over and over again. When he got up on stage, the drum beat stopped abruptly. There was no one there. The next day, his staff admitted that they'd also heard the phantom drummer playing late into the night.

A day or two after that, Bill caught sight of the ghost again. He had walked out onto the stage and spotted the ghost sitting in the audience, seven or eight rows from the front. Nearly as soon as he'd been spotted, the ghost vanished.

The shadowy ghost was not the only spirit to inhabit the Vogue Theatre, as Bill would soon learn. It was one week after he had given an informal tour of the theatre to a friend and his girlfriend — a tour he thought had been uneventful — that Bill learned of an unsettling encounter. Bill's friend told him that while they were on their tour, his girlfriend had seen a young man with dark hair and severe facial features sitting in an old chair in the projection booth. When they entered the booth, the young man had turned his head slowly and stared at the friend's girlfriend with a look of intense anger, and then he'd dissolved where he sat.

A few weeks later the same ghost nearly ruined a live performance of a show called *Unforgettable*. Bill was watching from the back of the house. One of the supporting actors, Shane McPherson, was on stage performing a song and dance number when he suddenly dropped his cane. Then he blew his dance steps and even a few lines from the song. During the intermission, Bill went downstairs, found Shane in his dressing room, and asked him what had happened.

The Vogue Theatre

"I don't know if you're going to believe what I'm about to tell you," Shane said.

After all the experiences he'd had in the theatre, Bill had a feeling he probably would.

While in the middle of his routine, Shane explained, he

had seen a young man with dark hair and sharp features walk through a fire exit near the front row at stage left. The young man stopped, looked directly into Shane's eyes, and then dissolved. Shane was so shocked by what he'd seen that he dropped his cane and messed up his performance.

Other staff members and performers have also had unusual experiences throughout the building. The day following Shane's encounter, technician David Raun was in charge of locking up the theatre for the night. As he passed the stage, he looked up and spotted a man standing in the doorway to the projection booth. He was standing in the shadows, but his face was clearly visible, and the dark hair and chiselled features matched the descriptions others had given of the ghost. Before David could do or say anything, the man disappeared.

An employee who worked in the theatre's box office was alone in the lobby one afternoon when all of a sudden she felt like she was no longer alone. She quickly turned and caught sight of a shadowy figure climbing the stairs to the balcony. When she checked, no one was there.

One night, after stacking advertising posters in the storage room, a group of employees locked up the theatre and went home. They returned in the morning to find the posters they'd so neatly stacked the day before strewn across the floor.

Another night singer Arnold Robinson walked downstairs to his dressing room when he was suddenly aware that someone — someone he couldn't see — was walking along beside him. He tried his best to ignore the presence, a remarkably hard thing to do, hopeful whoever it was would leave him alone once he entered his dressing room. It didn't.

Arnold mustered up all the courage he had and said, "If you want to hang out, that's cool." The spirit didn't take him up on his offer.

In the Vogue Theatre, the ghosts play on long after the curtain falls.

# THE DEAD MAN'S BED

## *Wakefield, Quebec*

Billy Brennan arrived in timber baron James Maclaren's camp in the late 1800s and was immediately assigned to sleep in a dead man's bed. That didn't give Billy pause. Every lumberjack knew that the job was dangerous and that death could come at any moment for any one of them, young or old, experienced or not. It was an accepted rule of the camps that when one lumberjack died, another would take his place with little delay or fanfare.

After his first long day on the job, Billy collapsed onto his bed, tired and sore. Sleep didn't come easy, however, and not just because cedar boughs served as his mattress. Before he was able to drift off, a man slowly approached his bunk and stared down at him. Then, without a word, the man yanked Billy's blanket off of him. Before Billy could ask the man why he had done that, the stranger disappeared.

The next day Billy shared the odd tale with some other men in the camp. After describing what the man looked like, everyone appeared to know who he was. Billy had been visited by the ghost of Long Jim Nesbitt.

Long Jim had drowned in the Gatineau River, a tragic yet common fate for many. White crosses can still be found along the shore, marking the locations where loggers drowned well over one hundred years ago.

Billy was understandably shocked by the news. It couldn't be so. Perhaps it had been his imagination. Perhaps it had been a dream.

That night, twice as tired and three times as sore as the day before, Billy once again laid down on his cedar mattress and hoped sleep would come quickly. But once again, the ghost of Long Jim Nesbitt appeared beside Billy's bed, stared down at him for a moment, yanked his blanket to the floor, and disappeared.

It happened again on the third night, the fourth and the fifth.

Billy, a tough man who had rarely been intimidated by anything in his young life, was growing incredibly scared. What did the ghost want? Why was he terrorizing him? And worst of all, what if his nighttime attacks became more threatening?

On his first day off since he'd taken the job at the camp, Billy walked north to the town of Farrellton. He hoped the village priest would know what to do. The trip took two and a half hours, but Billy would have walked it many times over if it brought him any resolution.

"I am being haunted by the ghost of the dead lad who used to sleep in my bunk," Billy told the priest. "The ghost of Long Jim Nesbitt is haunting me and I don't know why. But it is really scary and I can't go on much longer."

Fortunately for Billy, the priest provided some guidance. It seemed to him that the ghost had a specific reason for haunting Billy, and it might help to figure out what the dead man's reason was.

Billy thanked the priest and walked back to camp, mulling over the advice he'd received.

Night fell and the men shuffled off to their beds, and then to sleep. All but Billy. But this time at least he had a plan.

Without fail, the ghost appeared beside him. But before he could put one cold finger on the blanket, Billy leapt to his feet and demanded to know what the ghost wanted of him.

After a moment of deathly silence, the ghost spoke.

"Under your bottom blanket," he said in a slow, low hiss, "there is some money I owe to Charlie Farrell at Wakefield. I have been working all winter long to save the money to pay my debt. Will you please take the money to Charlie for me?" And without waiting for an answer, he disappeared.

Billy checked beneath the blanket under the cedar boughs and, sure enough, he found a secret stash of money. He didn't consider keeping it for himself, not for a second. When the sun rose the next morning he walked into town, inquired where he could find Charlie Farrell, and paid him the money.

The ghost of Long Jim Nesbitt never appeared in Maclaren's lumber camp again. His debt paid, he was finally able to rest in peace.

# THE CELLAR

## *Halifax, Nova Scotia*

Joanne Dolan was alone in the basement office of the Cellar Bar & Grill one night when the temperature suddenly plummeted. It wasn't the first time she'd experienced that — she'd felt inexplicable cold spots many times over the years — but it was the chilliest she'd ever felt it. She'd heard odd sounds and caught sight of things out of the corner of her eye before too, but had never seen anything like what she saw next. A misty form in the shape of a person passed through the room. It was a frightening sight that sent her running out of the office and up the stairs in a hurry. She needed to be around other people — *living* people.

Upstairs, she found three co-workers — Natalie, Barbara and Mike — and told them what had just happened to her.

Joanne then discovered she wasn't the only staff member who had had similar experiences.

On a quiet night not too long before, Natalie and Barbara were the only two people working after closing time. Natalie was clearing tables in the back dining room on the main floor, getting them set for the next day, while Barbara was upstairs closing up the bar. Other than the clinking sounds of the glasses and cutlery they were tidying, the restaurant was dead quiet.

"Natalie?" a voice called out.

"Be there in a minute," Natalie called upstairs, assuming it had been Barbara.

A few moments passed.

"Natalie?" the same voice said, and this time it sounded closer.

"I'm just out back checking glasses," Natalie said, growing a little annoyed by Barbara's intrusions. "I'll be right there."

A few more moments passed.

"Natalie?"

"Yes, Barbara," Natalie said with a sigh, giving up her work and leaving the back dining room. Barbara clearly wouldn't be ignored any longer.

But when Natalie asked Barbara what she wanted, Barbara shook her head and looked confused.

"I haven't been calling your name," Barbara replied.

Uncertain of who was in the restaurant with them — and what she wanted with Natalie — the two employees wrapped up their closing duties as quickly as possible and got out. They didn't feel comfortable being there a moment longer than necessary.

Mike Hubley, a chef at the restaurant, also noticed many things he couldn't explain over the years. It wasn't unusual for knives and other utensils to disappear when he'd turn his back for mere seconds. Often, when he was the only person in the building, he'd hear footsteps above him, see shadows moving out of the corner of his eye and, like Natalie, hear his name called out by an unseen presence. One morning he found a clipboard on the counter in the kitchen, even though he'd hung it on the wall the night before. He'd been the last one out of the building that night and the first one in in the morning.

Early one morning Mike saw a woman in an old-fashioned dress enter the dining room before the restaurant opened, so he approached her to let her know she'd have to leave and come back later. But when he got close to her she disappeared. Frightened, he called out to Joanne, who was also at work getting ready for the day. She rushed into the dining room. When she stepped into the spot where Mike had seen the ghost vanish, she noticed the temperature was incredibly cold, just like that day not too long before when she'd been in the basement office. It was so cold that she jumped backwards.

"Are you okay?" Mike asked her.

She nodded and made a decision. She was sick and tired of working in fear. Something needed to be done. Joanne summoned all her courage and stepped back into the cold spot.

"We aren't afraid of you," she said in the sternest voice she could summon.

At that moment the temperature immediately rose back

to normal. Her show of bravery had apparently worked.

Perhaps it had, but not forever.

Supernatural hijinks continued in the Cellar Bar & Grill. Salt and pepper shakers moved from table to table on their own, chairs switched places, computers went haywire, and fires in the fireplace were smothered out by invisible hands.

Joanne continued her attempts to get rid of the ghostly presence. One day she went downstairs to do inventory and felt an icy cold hand grab her shoulder from behind. She spun around but wasn't surprised to find no one there.

There are two theories regarding the restaurant's paranormal activity. In 1809 a woman named Elizabeth, who worked on a farm where the restaurant now stands, was murdered on the property. Her body was discovered the next day, but the culprit was not.

Another suspicion is that an unidentified woman whose body was discovered in a bag by the river behind the restaurant haunts the building. Mike Hubley's parents worked in the restaurant at the time and his father was the one to make the gruesome discovery. Unaware that the lumpy bag that had washed up on shore was a dead body, he opened it up and was horrified by what he found. The back door to the restaurant was open and the stench of the body was so potent that it filled the entire building. People noticed an increase in paranormal activity from that day on.

The Cellar Bar & Grill closed and reopened as Resto Urban Dining, and some say the ghost — or ghosts — left with the change. But others disagree, and current staff members have continued to report that the restaurant never seems completely empty.

Just as a rose by any other name would smell as sweet, a haunted restaurant by any other name would be as frightening.

# FOREVER AND EVER HOME

### Red Deer, Alberta

Elizabeth Plumtree, former executive director of the Red Deer Cultural Heritage Society, entered Cronquist House early one morning. It was a day like any other . . . or so she thought. She walked through the house on her way to turn off the alarm, but a loud sound stopped her cold.

*Fwump-fwump-fwump-fwump-fwump-fwump-fwump!*

Startled, she turned around and saw that the door between the butler's pantry and the dining room was swinging back and forth violently. It was moving too quickly to have been caused by anything other than someone passing through, so Elizabeth knew she wasn't alone in the house. But an unnerving thought entered her head and refused to leave: *No one can be in here because the alarm is still on.*

She turned off the alarm and searched the house, going from room to room, but it was completely empty. All the while she could hear the door swinging wildly, but when she returned to the dining room it suddenly stopped.

Built between 1911 and 1912 by Swedish immigrant Emmanuel Petterson Cronquist, a farmer and merchant who arrived in Alberta in 1893 with his family, Cronquist House stands out from the landscape like a classic haunted abode. Not surprisingly, the Queen Anne Revival style home, with a three-storey round turret and wrap-around verandah, is the setting for countless tales of ghostly goings-on.

Elias Cronquist was the home's final inhabitant. He died in the house in 1974. Considered by locals to be an eccentric recluse, Elias lived alone in the house for years and spent most of his time hidden away in one of the upstairs bedrooms. After his death, the Red Deer Cultural Heritage Society purchased the house and had it moved to its present location near Bower Ponds. That's when reports of paranormal activity first began to surface.

Staff members working alone in the building have heard Elias's loud, clomping footsteps from his bedroom above. From the sounds of his pacing, it appears as if he is angry. Elizabeth Plumtree believes he isn't pleased that his house was moved to a new location.

Elias is blamed for moving cups and saucers in the tea room when no one is looking. He slams doors and makes loud noises. Staff and visitors alike have reported chills and goosebumps on the backs of their necks, a sure sign that Elias is standing right behind them.

*The Cronquist family, between 1910 and 1915*

One day, when a new employee had just started work, there was a huge crash from an empty room that startled him greatly; Elizabeth tried to calm him down by explaining that it was just Elias. Whether or not that made the new employee feel better or worse is unknown.

Some days Elias isn't in as foul a mood and has been known to approach people sitting outside on the front porch and strike up a conversation. At first the unsuspecting visitors believe the man to be alive and well. But when the man suddenly disappears, leaving behind no trace that he had been there at all, they become frightfully aware that they were just in the company of the long-dead Elias.

A girl named Auriel was hanging out in Bower Ponds late one night with her best friend. The girls had heard the ghost stories from Cronquist House and wanted to see for themselves if there was any truth to them. Not yet convinced that the house was actually haunted, they were completely shocked (and a little frightened) when they looked up at the turret window and saw the ghost of Elias staring down at them disapprovingly.

Based on all of the evidence, it appears that Elias just wants to be left alone in the house he never wanted to leave. But as the Red Deer Cultural Heritage Society continues to operate out of the building, hosting high tea and giving historical tours, that's one wish he won't be granted anytime soon.

# THEY FEED ON FEAR

## St. Vincent, Alberta

It was 3:30 a.m. and Margo Lagasse heard the footsteps on the roof again. The phantom sound had woken her every night for a week. Something needed to be done.

Margo and her sons had just moved into the new home they had had built on a bluff overlooking St. Vincent Lake, surrounded by trees and solitude. There wasn't a neighbour within sight and the house was anything but conventional. A man had owed the Lagasse family a great deal of money but was unable to repay his debt. What he did have was a large stash of concrete blocks, and Margo decided to accept them instead of money. She used them to build a castle in the woods. It didn't take the family long to realize something was amiss in their new home.

Like clockwork, Margo woke up every night at the same

time to the sound of loud footsteps above her head. The disturbance had begun earlier in the week. At first she had assumed it was one of her sons walking around — their rooms were above hers. But when she checked, she had found them asleep in their beds. The footsteps weren't coming from within the house. They were coming from the roof.

Nearing her wits' end, Margo finally built up the courage to climb out onto the roof to investigate. There was no one there. The footsteps returned the next night and the next and the next, until Margo lost her cool and yelled at whoever was out there, commanding him to stop. Whatever was out there quit walking on the roof at night, but it didn't go away for good.

A few nights later her sons had some friends over. As they hung out listening to music, they heard an unseen presence come down the stairs, the entire staircase shaking with each hollow-sounding footfall. The spirit had entered the house.

The boys bolted for the safety of one of their bedrooms and locked themselves in. They were unable to calm down, however, since they could hear many voices talking in the room beside them, despite the fact that they were the only people in the house.

Some time later, one of the boys had his first sighting of a ghost. He was sitting on a couch near the base of the staircase when he saw a blond woman wearing a long dress float down the steps and beckon at him to follow her. Needless to say, he didn't.

Maybe it was this woman who attacked Tim Landru,

a local handyman. Tim helped Margo with the castle's upkeep. One day as he was walking upstairs, a hand reached out and grabbed the back of his knee. Terrified, he raced up the rest of the stairs, only to find there was no one behind him when he reached the top — no one visible, that is.

As haunted as the castle was, the woods that surround it were even scarier. Although no one had ever seen what lurked in the bushes, everyone knew it was big. Both Margo and Tim heard something charging at them through the trees, something that sounded as large as a moose. But then, just when it seemed like the attacker was going to break through the trees and trample them to death, it disappeared.

One day, determined not to be afraid of something he couldn't see, Tim stood up to the noise. The sound didn't rush at him. That's when he and Margo started to believe that the ghosts fed on fear, and that standing up to them made them go away.

At least for a short while. Then they came back.

As more houses were built near Margo's home, more people became acquainted with the strange goings-on within. One evening, Margo heard guitar music coming from upstairs, so she ran outside and told her neighbours. A few people approached the house and heard the same music, but all refused to enter. No one wanted to come face to face with the phantom musician. That doesn't mean they didn't enjoy the music the ghost played. On one occasion, neighbours reported to Margo that they'd heard organ music coming from the house while she was away.

It was absolutely lovely, they reported. No one had been in the house, and there had never been an organ in it either.

A less desirable result of living with ghosts was the foul odour — the smell of burning flesh — that often rose out of nowhere. It would seep into bread if loaves were left out for more than an hour, making them inedible. Margo's mother refused to return to the house because of the stench. It didn't go away until Margo offered a young priest to use her home for a retreat. He didn't say whether or not he had performed an exorcism while he'd stayed there, but he did make a point of letting Margo know that he had performed many exorcisms in the past.

Even if the priest did perform an exorcism, it only got rid of the awful smell, not the ghosts. One night, before bed, Margo wrote a note to the spirits and left it on a table beneath a lamp. The next morning she awoke to discover something had shattered the lampshade.

And then one night, Margo finally saw one of the ghosts herself. She woke up suddenly and saw a familiar-looking man with a moustache standing beside her bed, staring at her in silence. He soon disappeared, but he returned a few more nights until Margo realized why he looked familiar. He was a local man who had died a short while before, and Margo knew his mother.

"What do you want?" Margo asked.

"Go to my mother," the dead man said, "and tell her I'm happy where I am."

At first Margo didn't go visit his mother, who wasn't a very nice person. But after the man interrupted her sleep a few more times, Margo decided she wouldn't get any rest until she carried out the ghost's bidding. The next day she travelled to the nearby town of St. Paul and knocked on the old woman's door. As soon as the woman opened the door, Margo passed along the message and left without waiting a moment longer.

That night the man appeared one final time. He gave Margo a warm smile and then vanished in a cloud of smoke, never to return.

In the years since, Margo has researched the history of the land her castle was built on but hasn't uncovered anything that explains why it might be haunted. Perhaps it has nothing to do with the property and everything to do with the style of home she built. After all, every castle, even one built with cinder blocks, needs a ghost.

# THE OTHER SIDE

## *Burnaby, British Columbia*

Chris Dixon was two years old the day he told his parents that he had two new friends. Their names, the boy said, were Kukin and Frindon, and they had appeared in his room in the middle of the night.

Dave and Patricia, Chris's parents, knew that Kukin and Frindon were imaginary. Inventing playmates, especially among preschool children, is common, nothing to fear or be concerned about. But as the days went on and Chris told them more about his two new nighttime friends, Dave and Patricia began to grow concerned. Soon their concerns turned into full-fledged fear.

They had moved into their small, two-bedroom bungalow in a northern suburb of Burnaby before Chris was born. The house was very old, and in the 1930s a large family with fourteen children had lived there, all crammed in together. The Dixons had looked forward to one day raising children of their own there.

Though the Dixons were happy in their bungalow, the second bedroom gave them a bad vibe that they couldn't quite explain. The room was noticeably chillier than the rest of the house and they felt as though they were being watched in there — as if something was lurking in the closet, hiding under the bed or peering out of the shadows. Thanks in part to this unsettling feeling, Patricia would often wake her husband in the middle of the night, certain that someone must have broken into their house. Time after time, Dave would dutifully investigate his wife's concerns, and time after time, he would find the house to be completely empty.

Chris slept in a crib in his parents' bedroom until he was two, at which point it was decided that he was old enough to move into the second bedroom and sleep on his own. But he wouldn't actually be sleeping on his own.

Kukin and Frindon visited three or four nights a week. At first it seemed innocent enough, but that quickly changed as Chris revealed more details about his friends' behaviour.

The imaginary friends refused to appear while Dave and Patricia were still awake. They waited for everyone in the house to be asleep and then they woke Chris. His father asked Chris how they appeared each night.

"They walk through the wall," Chris said.

Dave asked where the two friends came from.

"The other side," Chris said.

"The other side of what?"

"The river," the boy answered.

Dave and Patricia shared a concerned look. They didn't live anywhere near a river. There was no way he would have made up something like that. As alarming as that was, it couldn't hold a candle to the tidbit Chris shared with his parents next. He told them that every night Kukin and Frindon asked Chris to go with them, through the wall and over the river to the other side.

Fearing that Chris's life was in danger, Dave and Patricia warned their son to never, *ever* go anywhere with Kukin and Frindon.

The two friends continued to visit most nights. They persisted in trying to get Chris to pass over to the other side. Chris obeyed his parents and refused to go anywhere with Kukin and Frindon. They only finally left the poor boy alone when he was three years old and the Dixons moved to a new house.

Early in the morning after their first night in the new home, Dave and Patricia asked Chris what Kukin and Frindon thought of his new bedroom.

"They had to stay at the old house," the boy said. "They couldn't leave."

The Dixons had seen the last of Kukin and Frindon, but Kukin and Frindon hadn't seen the last of the old, two-bedroom bungalow. Two young men moved in after the Dixons, but they didn't stay long.

The man who moved into Chris's old room could never get a decent night's sleep. Everything seemed normal when he went to bed, but he'd wake up in the middle of the night with the feeling that something was watching him. This happened every night until the man couldn't take it anymore. Instead he began sleeping on a recliner in the living room. That wasn't a permanent solution, however. One night, after a few nights of undisturbed sleep, he awoke sometime after midnight. From where he lay in the recliner he could see into the darkness of his bedroom. Standing within it, staring out at him, were two shadowy figures the size of young boys. Thinking that a couple of kids had snuck into the house through an unlocked window, he leapt from the recliner and ran into the bedroom, but it was empty. The two boys had disappeared, and there were no signs of any intrusion.

The two men moved out of the bungalow the very next day.

When the Dixons first heard this they weren't surprised. They'd been driven out of the bungalow themselves, although not quite as quickly as the two men. And although they can't prove it, Dave and Patricia are certain that Kukin and Frindon still haunt the Burnaby house. After all, the two ghosts might be from the other side, but they can never leave.

# PHOTO CREDITS

Joel A. Sutherland is an author and librarian. He is the author of several books in the Haunted Canada series, as well as *Be a Writing Superstar, Summer's End* and Haunted, a series of middle-grade horror novels. His short fiction has appeared in many anthologies and magazines, alongside the likes of Stephen King and Neil Gaiman. He has been a juror for the John Spray Mystery Award and the Monica Hughes Award for Science Fiction and Fantasy.

He appeared as "The Barbarian Librarian" on the Canadian edition of the hit television show *Wipeout,* making it all the way to the third round and proving that librarians can be just as tough and crazy as anyone else.

Joel lives with his family in southeastern Ontario, where he is always on the lookout for ghosts.

# HAUNTED CANADA

Read the whole chilling series.

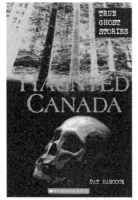

978-0-7791-1410-8

978-0-439-96122-6

978-0-439-93777-1

978-1-4431-2893-3

978-1-4431-3929-8

978-1-4431-4878-8

978-1-4431-4881-8

978-1-4431-4883-2